ANTAGONISTS' COOKBOOK

VOL. 2

© 2022 Marcus V. Calvert

By Tales Unlimited, LLC.

Cover by Adam Fields

Edited by Ed Buchanan

Acknowledgments

*I'd like to thank Ed Buchanan for beating this one
into shape.*

*Adam Fields, thank you're the awesome book
cover.*

*To everyone else who had a hand in this twisted
thing being written (living or not), I thank you.*

*I must also tip a hat to my fellow artists and
strangers-turned-fans. You truly are a hip crowd.*

QUICK INSTRUCTIONS

Every character has seven attributes: Speed, Endurance, Might, Intellect, Will, Alertness, and Health. Each attribute comes in three levels: human, superhuman, and beyond superhuman.

Super powers (typically) have two levels: superhuman and beyond superhuman.

Any power with a "#" in front of it means that it's a character power (like a killer, genius, alien, etc.).

This book has 200 "Recipes" (or templates) with five "Ingredients" (or super powers) each. These super powers are short, sweet, and flexibly vague. Set them up as you see fit, for whatever story you're out to tell, then fill in the details.

The system works best when you have a general idea of the character you want—from a witch to a psychic to a hostile alien.

To begin, randomly flip to a Recipe page and pick the power(s) best suited for the character type in your head. Jot down the Recipe and Ingredient numbers, then flip to another random page. Repeat the process until you're satisfied. Try not to pick more than five powers— unless you're shooting for a boss-level character.

Then list them accordingly. *Factor in the attributes and powers—then set the details of both.* Don't be afraid of details. The better you know your antagonist(s), the better you know your story.

SAMPLER ONE:
A DIFFERENT TYPE OF CURSED SWORD

Let's say you wanted to create a different type of cursed sword. Something that needs to be snatched from a murderous villain and locked away. What is it and how does it work?

Put a few of the common traits in your head, like:

*Magical sword
*Near-indestructible
*Cuts through almost anything

Flip to that first random Recipe. For this example, I ended up at "Recipe #322 – Primal Cutlet." I looked through the (five) Ingredients and found two that I liked:

2 - This power allows you to talk to beasts and (usually) control them.

5 - You can turn someone into an animal or a mutated variant of one. Set the details.

It's a start.
With a stab (or even a cut), you can turn your enemies into squealing hogs and feed them to the poor. You can turn your minions into hawkmen scouts or minotaur bodyguards.

If you run into a pack of wolves, you could make them slaughter each other (for giggles). Perhaps you turn some ladies into mermaids and "persuade" them to scavenge the ocean floor for sunken treasures.

How long does this bestial touch last? Let's make it a three-day thing. Does the sword work on you? Nah.

I'll flip ahead to "Recipe #373 – Sweet Pepper Minion." Hm. Not much there:

1 - #You're meaner than most people. Boost your Endurance and Will attributes to superhuman capacity.

The longer you wield the sword, the crueler (and tougher) you become. It's a logical outcome for a cursed blade—and useful in a fight.

I'll flip to "Recipe #298 – Minestrone Sound Monster." Now things get interesting . . .

3 - #Whatever you are, you can't pass for a human. Boost two of your human-scale attributes to superhuman capacity. Set the details on what kind of creature you are.

5 - #You're a truly evil monster who must feed upon the living to survive. Boost two of your human-scale attributes to superhuman capacity.

Stack these five powers and a backstory emerges:

Once upon a time, a man was cursed to walk the world as a hideous monster. He became a fearsome warlord, fed upon the living, and certain powers (see above) emerged.
    Eventually, some lucky soul chopped him down with this very sword. That should've been that. Instead, his blood stained the weapon and won't wash off. Anyone who wields it long enough will fall under the curse's

sway, go very dark, and slowly turn into that evil beast—
with ambitions of conquest.

No one's lasted long enough to fully turn. Legends
suggest that if someone can harness the full power of the
curse, he (or she) could evolve even more powers—and
possibly become a forest deity. Maybe that's why
wielders of this blade tend to surround themselves with
minions—only to get murdered anyway.

After all, it is a cursed sword.

I stopped here and worked on the attributes, powers, and details.

As long as the wielder is even *near* that sword, six of the seven attributes are at superhuman levels. Only the Intellect attribute is human-scale (unless a super genius ends up a wielder). Thus, you've got a physically dominant monster with heightened senses and a rock-hard mind. Someone who could, in time, ascend to godhood.

SAMPLER TWO:
A DIFFERENT TYPE OF ROGUE SPY

One of the world's top spies goes rogue. Let's start with the logical core of the idea:

*A skilled spy, who's saved the world a time or twenty.
*Well-known, respected, and feared in espionage circles.
*Gadgets (naturally).

Now, let's go random. I flipped to "Recipe #279 – Hot-smoked Scoundrel."

1 - #You are stunningly attractive and/or charismatic, which allows you to convince people to do whatever you want (at superhuman capacity).

2 - #Somehow, you're very wealthy (probably with billions to your name).

Interesting. Now, why would a rich and charming person get into the intelligence trade?

I flipped to "Recipe #350 – Smoked Cult Leader" and picked:

1 - #Whether you're a genius or just pretty quick-witted, you often make very good decisions—to the point where people tend to follow you.

4 - You have access to a loyal group of combat-hardened minions. Give them gear and an origin story (hired mercs, temporary conjurations, members of your tribe, etc.).

I decided to do another . . . and came up with "Recipe #328 – Rage Drug Ribs." Nah. The powers didn't fit. [Author's Note: It's okay to scrap it and move on. It's your story, remember?]

Then I flipped to "Recipe #239 – Dairy Free Tribal Kid." One of them adds spice to this rogue agent:

5 - You always find whatever you need to achieve your objective(s). Too bad having the right tools doesn't guarantee success.

This last power would apply to all levels of need. From finding a useful blunt object in a bar fight to devising a way to bring a global superpower to its knees.

Oh my! A resourceful mastermind with minions and superspy training . . .

What if your parents were criminal masterminds with a global syndicate? They were such a threat that an intelligence agency had them killed. You survived. Loyal minions faked your death and raised you to avenge your parents.

Perhaps one of the minions oversaw the restoration of your parent's syndicate. Your identity was scrubbed clean and you managed to infiltrate that intelligence agency (as a mole). You earned their trust, rose through the ranks, and erased other evil masterminds in the process.

This lead minion eventually got greedy and decided to use you like a disposable chess piece. When you didn't die in the field, he (or she) decided to have you killed. Attempts were made on your life. Thanks to a few loyal supporters, you survived and killed this traitor.

The cool part's that you secured your birthright without your spy bosses having a clue. You eventually learned the identities of those responsible for your parents' deaths. Then you concocted an elegant revenge scheme and ordered your minions to carry it out.

As current and former agency members ended up dead, you're sent out to investigate! You happily stay one step behind your kill teams. The last target's the agent who pulled the trigger on your parents.

You're tasked with his protection. While an old drunk, the retired agent managed to survive the first attempt. Rather than let him escape, you killed him with your bare hands.

Sadly, your cover's blown and a kill order's out on you. No matter. You now run one of the most dangerous criminal organizations on the planet. Most of your competitors are dead. You've got money, minions, and all kinds of stolen agency intel.

Time to play . . .

I stopped here and worked on the attributes, powers, and details.

All seven of the spy's attributes are human-scale. Still, this rogue agent might be good enough to kill super heroes (on a good day). The rationale? Experience, elite skill sets, resources, willing minions, and gadgetry would level the playing field. The rogue might even have super villains on the payroll—for a rainy day.

DETAILED INSTRUCTIONS

As previously mentioned, this system comes with 200 "Recipes." Each is a pre-generated character template. Within each template are five powers that come together (like "Ingredients" in a meal) to create that Recipe.

1. This system works best if you have a vague idea of your antagonist in mind (say, a ninja or witch). Then you flip to a random page and find a power(s) that suits that character. Scribble down its Recipe number and Ingredient number(s).

2. Is your character done? If so, stop. If not, flip to another random page. This time, your selections are based on the character and any power(s) already selected. The goal is to create a "whole" character without stacking in too many powers. With each choice, scribble down the Recipe and Ingredient numbers (for future reference).

3. How many powers should a character have? Try 1-3 powers for a minor character and 4-5 powers for major characters within your story. In the end, it's up to you.

NOTE: During the generation process, it's okay to replace one (or multiple) selected power(s) if you find something better. Sometimes it is the best way to move forward!

4. At some point, you'll find a Recipe page where none of the powers listed align with your fledgling

antagonist. That's fine. You can either continue to another page . . . or treat it as a possible stopping point.

5. The only time I'd recommend going for plenty of powers is if you're designing a genuinely dangerous character. Maybe it's a boss-level super villain, a sentient starship, or a disinterested gambling deity in Chapter Nine of your current novel. The odd thing about this process though? You might be able to destroy the world with *just one power*. Keep that in mind.

6. Try to think up "different" combinations of powers. Stuff powers together people don't see very often (if ever). Imagine a cursed sword that steals a bit of your morality with every cut (or that adds it). Or a shapeshifting gorgon with a mutagenic bite. With a clever merging of powers, you'll have unforgettable foes and threats for your protagonist.

7. Once you've finalized your picks, flesh out the attributes, powers, and details.

8. "Capacity" and "attributes" will be mentioned throughout the power listings. What do they mean?

CAPACITY: Think of this as a measure of impact. This system has three capacities (or scales): human, superhuman, and beyond superhuman. A weapon might have a "human" scale (like a knife, sword, or grenade), a "superhuman" scale (like a mystical axe or artillery barrage), or go "beyond superhuman" (like a megaton nuke or a deity's full wrath).

Superhuman abilities and attributes are beyond those of normal humans. A super genius is smarter than a genius. Someone with superhuman strength can easily toss cars around. Going "beyond superhuman" means that an ability has been boosted to freakish levels—even among superhumans.

NOTE: The only time a super power should be in the human scale is if it's barely functioning (perhaps because of a power negation device, an adversary's curse, etc.).

ATTRIBUTES: This system has seven attributes for each character:

Speed – How fast/agile/precise you are.

Endurance – How long you can function without sustenance or rest. It's also a measure of pain tolerance.

Might – How strong you are. If you want to put a maximum lifting capacity to a character's strength, suit yourself. Superhuman capacity starts where maximum human capacity ends. Beyond superhuman starts wherever you want it to (100 tons, 1,000 tons, etc.).

Intellect – How smart you are.

Will – Mental strength and resilience.

Alertness – How perceptive you are.

Health – How much damage your body can handle before you die.

NOTE: The difference between Endurance and Health is a peculiar one. Someone with a superhuman Endurance (but a human-scale Health attribute) has mad stamina and a great pain tolerance—but might die from a well-placed wound. Now flip this around. Someone with human Endurance and superhuman Health would tire quickly, have a glass jaw, but could still survive an obscene amount of damage.

Unless you're creating a superhuman character (like an alpha vampire), assume that all starting characters have human-scale attributes. If you want to boost them later (as a tweak or plot development), feel free. But at the beginning, treat them like regular people: then give them powers and see what changes.

IN CONCLUSION . . .

Whether setting up a fight scene, designing weaponry, or cooking up sub-races for a fantasy series, the *Antagonists' Cookbook* will save you a ton of time, boring results, and wrong turns. This system will help you create intriguing enemies for that awesome hero(ine) of yours.

Lastly, should you use this guide to create your protagonist? **No. Never. <u>A protagonist should come from you and you alone.</u>** *The Antagonists' Cookbook* is meant to design everyone else in your story. Enjoy.

RECIPES

Recipe #201 – Agromorphic Pizza

1 - #You're a truly evil monster who must feed upon the living to survive. Boost two of your human-scale attributes to superhuman capacity.

2 - Most physical impacts and projectiles harmlessly pass through you (like you're made of mud). Set the details, including which attacks can hurt you.

3 - You can turn dead plant matter into devices and weapons (without changing the original look). Think "apple grenade" or "banana phone."

4 - You can turn people, animals, or plants into different kinds of plant-based lifeforms. Are they carnivorous?

5 - You can shoot razor-sharp shards. What (one) material are they made of? Feel free to mix this power with any others you might have.

Recipe #202 – Ahi Tuna Warhorse

1 - You own a very special mount with a mind of its own and one free power. Feel free to mix this power with any others you might have.

2 - #While you may take damage normally, only a handful of things can truly kill you. Boost your Will, Endurance, or Health attribute to superhuman capacity.

3 - You can track a target (by scent alone) from miles away.

4 - You can establish two-way, telepathic communications with anyone in your line of sight.

5 - You kick with a skill that's beyond superhuman.

Recipe #203 – Alchemical Cop Slushie

1 - #You have a superhuman flair for finding people and solving mysteries—whether you're a spy, lawman, freelance sleuth, or someone's pet enforcer.

2 - You have access to a reliable network of allies within business, government, and other legitimate sectors of society.

3 - You can use water for scrying (spying) purposes.

4 - #You're an alchemist with a finite number of potion formulas in your head. While they take time and materials to brew up, each potion's a temporary "power in a bottle." Set the perks and limitations.

5 - You have armor-piercing projectiles that can pump a desired drug/toxin into a target.

Recipe #204 – Alien Abductor Salad

1 - #You can copy the appearance and voices of other humanoid beings.

2 - #You are (or were) a spy, with a superhuman skill set.

3 - #You have alien blood in your veins. Boost two of your attributes to superhuman capacity.

4 - You're an expert in almost everything alien (from cultures to languages to weaponry), with a skill level that's beyond superhuman.

5 - You have access to a portal designed for interstellar travel.

Recipe #205 – Angus Space-time Cannon

1 - You can fire a projectile that explodes on impact. Is the damage lethal or non-lethal?

2 - You have a unique, feature-loaded vehicle (from a spy car to an attack sub to a star cruiser).

3 - You have access to a portal designed for interstellar travel.

4 - You've got a weapon of mass destruction: something with an effect that's beyond superhuman. Does it have to be lethal? No. Just know that it's overwhelmingly powerful. Feel free to mix other power(s) with it, then set the details.

5 - You can open a portal to any point in the past or future.

Recipe #206 – Apple Cider Psi-suit

1 - Your costume and/or uniform counts as lightweight body armor. Feel free to mix this power with any others you might have.

2 - You have a precision, long-range psychic beam that inflicts superhuman damage. Set the details.

3 - You can move solid objects, either via telekinesis or some kind of tractor beam.

4 - You have some kind of sensor tech that functions at superhuman capacity.

5 - A superhuman-capacity defense protects your mind against psychic attacks.

Recipe #207 – Avocado Mind Scrambler

1 - You can indefinitely switch the minds of other beings, at superhuman capacity.

2 - You can reflect any psychic power or attack back to its point of origin. Is this power flexible enough to allow benign mental contact to get through?

3 - Somehow, you can view a target (surroundings and all) from up to a certain range. Is this astral projection, magic, or something else? If relevant, you can mix this power with other abilities.

4 - You can switch bodies with another being. What are the mechanics/limitations of this power?

5 - #You are—or were—a professional villain. Pick up a criminal skill specialty that you can utilize, with superhuman capacity.

Recipe #208 – Baby Back Blissmonger

1 - You can release an area-effect field of temporary, paralytic bliss (which might be addictive to your targets).

2 - You're almost immune to all of your other powers (should they ever be used on you or somehow misfire).

3 - Until it stops, intense pleasure will boost ALL of your human stats to superhuman.

4 - You have your very own pocket dimension. Assign the rules, perks, and drawbacks to such a place.

5 - Get near someone enjoying intense pleasure and any of your injuries will heal by the second.

Recipe #209 – Balsamic Hypno-assassin

1 - #You're a well-versed killer. Your talents can be merely human or at superhuman capacity.

2 - You can heal from most injuries within a few minutes.

3 - If you wish, technological devices can't detect you—from cameras to high-end sensors.

4 - #You've mastered a non-mystical fighting style, which allows you to fight with superhuman capacity.

5 - Your voice can hypnotize targets, at superhuman capacity.

Recipe #210 – Banished Elf Grits

1 - #You have a superhuman flair for finding people and solving mysteries—whether you're a spy, lawman, freelance sleuth, or someone's pet enforcer.

2 - In your hands, any mundane weapon inflicts superhuman mystical damage. The effect ends right after you let the weapon go.

3 - Your skill with thrown weapons is beyond superhuman.

4 - #You can cast spells. How that works is up to you. Boost your Will attribute to superhuman capacity.

5 - #You have enough elven blood to get the perks (attributes, longevity, etc.).

Recipe #211 – Battle Drone Queso

1 - You can turn parts of your body into whatever small weaponry you wish. Set the details and limitations. Feel free to merge this ability with any other relevant power(s).

2 - You can design and build NON-MYSTICAL weapons beyond superhuman capacity. Doesn't mean you're deadly in a gunfight, though.

3 - You can reflect mundane energy attacks at a scale that's beyond superhuman. It won't work on magic or psychics. Set the details.

4 - #You're some kind of robot. Boost three of your attributes to superhuman capacity.

5 - Your battle armor protects you from damage and raises your Might attribute to superhuman capacity. What other features does it have? Feel free to merge another power(s) with this one.

Recipe #212 – Battle Giant Hummus

1 - #You can grow to a certain height. Set the details (both for yourself and anything you have on you). If you want to be permanently large, that's fine too.

2 - You can make objects grow.

3 - Normally, it takes two actions to draw a weapon and then use it. Well, you're so fast that you can make it count as one action. If feasible, this advantage can also be applied to another power(s).

4 - #You have extensive military experience and a natural affinity with any kind of weapon. Also, boost one of your attributes to superhuman capacity.

5 - Your skin self-hardens (like armor) just before anything harmful can hit you.

Recipe #213 – Beastshifter Cupcakes

1 - #Whatever you are, you can't pass for a human. Boost two of your human-scale attributes to superhuman capacity. Set the details on what kind of creature you are.

2 - You can turn into any non-mystical animal.

3 - As long as you're moving around, incoming attacks tend to miss you. This power works at superhuman capacity—even on attacks you don't see coming. Of course, some attacks can't be dodged.

4 - #Your skills at wilderness combat, survival, and tracking are at superhuman capacity.

5 - During a fight, you'll be able to ignore your injuries (from broken bones to fatal wounds) until the fight's over—then it'll all catch up to you. Note: certain injuries will still kill you on the spot (like decapitation or a nuke blast).

Recipe #214 – Beef Brawling Alien

1 - #You have alien blood in your veins. Boost two of your attributes to superhuman capacity.

2 - You've got some kind of edged attack that's a part of you (claws, horns, fangs, etc.).

3 - Think of your tongue as an extendable weapon. The range, damage type(s), and other details are up to you.

4 - You have an unarmed fighting skill that's beyond superhuman.

5 - You can maneuver and fight by sound alone.

Recipe #215 – Beer-battered Zombie Maker

1 - #You've got demonic blood in you. Pick up one extra power and boost two of your attributes to superhuman. Now, what kind of demon are you?

2 - You have more than two legs. If you want to make them something else (like tentacles), feel free.

3 - You can turn living beings into zombies. Also, feel free to mix this ability with another power(s).

4 - Your deafening, NON-LETHAL sonic wail can shatter glass, knock people unconscious, and damage their hearing. Set the details.

5 - Your bite can inflict superhuman damage and might actually be stronger than you are.

Recipe #216 – Boneless Merc Boss

1 - You have a small arsenal of offensive and/or defensive gadgetry.

2 - You have a unique, feature-loaded vehicle (from a spy car to an attack sub to a star cruiser).

3 - #You're a genetic superhuman (born or augmented) with one free power and one superhuman attribute.

4 - #You have a superhuman flair for finding people and solving mysteries—whether you're a spy, lawman, freelance sleuth, or someone's pet enforcer.

5 - You have access to a loyal group of combat-hardened minions. Give them gear and an origin story (hired mercs, temporary conjurations, members of your tribe, etc.).

Recipe #217 – Bouncing Telekinetic Kingfish

1 - You can safely ricochet off solid objects and inflict (up to) superhuman damage. Aside from combat, this also makes for a decent form of transportation.

2 - Most people can do one action at a time. You can do up to three. However, two of those actions must be non-violent.

3 - You can look at an object and know its structural status (including weak spots).

4 - You can heal from most injuries within a few minutes.

5 - You can move solid objects, either via telekinesis or some kind of tractor beam.

Recipe #218 – Braised Psi-witch

1 - #You can cast spells. How that works is up to you. Boost your Will attribute to superhuman capacity.

2 - #You have enough telepathic DNA to read surface thoughts (at superhuman capacity). Replace one of your other powers with something psychic—if you want to.

3 - You can read and/or copy a target's memories, at superhuman capacity.

4 - Establish some form of contact and you can alter a target's memories.

5 - From miles out, you can establish two-way telepathic contact with a handful of minds. Feel free to merge this power with other relevant abilities.

Recipe #219 – Breaded Spectral Speedster

1 - #You're a speedster, which allows you to move at superhuman capacity (and probably faster than sound).

2 - You can make intangible spirits and mystical entities solid—either as a favor or to better fight them. Is this a temporary effect? Can you use this power on yourself? Set the details.

3 - #You're old, wise, and can move like a prime athlete.

4 - Your costume and/or uniform counts as lightweight body armor. Feel free to mix this power with any others you might have.

5 - #You're some kind of spectral entity (from a murdered soul to a possessive demon). Define your origins, strengths, and weaknesses.

Recipe #220 – Bully Salad w/ Apple Slices

1 - #You're a remarkable kid. How is up to you. Pick one attribute and boost it to superhuman capacity.

2 - #Your sonic attack inflicts sound-based and kinetic-force damage. Is it a yell, weapon, or something else? Feel free to merge it with other (relevant) powers/weapons.

3 - Stomp on a flat surface and some kind of barrier wall appears. What's it made of?

4 - Your lungs allow you to carry a note/scream/breath attack for several minutes and even hold your breath for hours at a time.

5 - #You're meaner than most people. Boost your Endurance and Will attributes to superhuman capacity.

Recipe #221 – Caesar Salad Rager

    1 - Your insults (no matter how trite) attack the mind with superhuman ability. Those who can't resist will drop everything and attack you.

    2 - The presence of rage (either yours or someone else's) will temporarily boost your human-level attributes to superhuman capacity.

    3 - #You've got demonic blood in you. Pick up one extra power and boost two of your attributes to superhuman. Now, what kind of demon are you?

    4 - In the presence of someone else's rage, you'll heal by the second.

    5 - Win a one-on-one fight and your defeated foe will feel pain whenever you want—until there's a rematch and you lose.

Recipe #222 – Candied Hell Minion

1 - You answer to someone (or something) with a lot of useful connections and influence. This individual can ease your path, save your life, or have you killed for too many failures.

2 - You're well-versed in summoning mystical creatures (from other planes of existence).

3 - #Whether you're a genius or just pretty quick-witted, you often make very good decisions—to the point where people tend to follow you.

4 - You've got an indestructible (mystical) item/weapon that'll return to you from anywhere. When wielding it, any feats you make are in the superhuman range. Any powers you merge with it will go beyond superhuman capacity.

5 - #You're an anointed follower of a higher (or darker) power. Boost either your Will or Intellect to superhuman capacity. Needless to say, your prayers tend to get answered quickly (but in strange and mysterious ways).

Recipe #223 – Canned Prankster God

1 - You always find whatever you need to achieve your objective(s). Too bad having the right tools doesn't guarantee success.

2 - If you selfishly retreat from a threat (without regard for anyone else), you'll always escape.

3 - You can persuade folks to do things your way with superhuman capacity.

4 - Until they see you in action, people tend to ignore and underestimate you.

5 - #You're a fledgling/lesser god, who can (to some extent) bend reality on a whim.

Recipe #224 – Cheddar Chive Time Merc

1 - You have hundreds of skills in your head (maybe more).

2 - You have a small arsenal of offensive and/or defensive gadgetry.

3 - You have access to a loyal group of combat-hardened minions. Give them gear and an origin story (hired mercs, temporary conjurations, members of your tribe, etc.).

4 - You can open a portal to any point in the past or future.

5 - #You were born in a vastly different time period (past or future). Set the backstory.

Recipe #225 – Chef Cursemonger Cups

1 - You've mastered a number of potent curse enchantments that can be inflicted upon your targets.

2 - You're famous (in a good way), which can come in handy—if you play your cards right.

3 - #You're a well-versed killer. Your talents can be merely human or at superhuman capacity.

4 - No matter how careless you are with your secret identity, no one can figure it out unless you intentionally reveal it.

5 - You have an extensive network of reliable criminal contacts.

Recipe #226 – Childless Witch Minestrone

1 - #You can cast spells. How that works is up to you. Boost your Will attribute to superhuman capacity.

2 - You have easy access to a vast amount of previously stored information (what kind is up to you).

3 - #You are stunningly attractive and/or charismatic, which allows you to convince people to do whatever you want (at superhuman capacity).

4 - You can automatically detect the presence of magic, within a certain range.

5 - You can survive dangers and heal from anything within a day—as long as you don't have any kids.

Recipe #227 – Chili Dipped Bounty Hunter

1 - You have a non-lethal energy attack that will stun humans and most superhumans.

2 - #You have a superhuman flair for finding people and solving mysteries—whether you're a spy, lawman, freelance sleuth, or someone's pet enforcer.

3 - You have some kind of kinetic beam attack. No, it doesn't do heat or explosive damage. It just pokes a hole through whatever it can penetrate.

4 - You can emit a directed energy beam that will negate a single target's innate super powers (if any). Set the details.

5 - For better or worse, your name is feared far and wide. Set the pros and cons of having such an infamous rep.

Recipe #228 – Chrono Grifter Ramen

1 - You can persuade folks to do things your way with superhuman capacity.

2 - #You're a powerful minion (with perks) who answers to Time. Pick up two extra powers that will help with your duties.

3 - #Whether you're a genius or just pretty quick-witted, you often make very good decisions—to the point where people tend to follow you.

4 - Establish contact and you can "drink" your victims' memories and skills away by the second.

5 - X number of times per day, you can freeze time over a localized area. Set the details and downside(s) for this power.

Recipe #229 – City-killer Nanobomb w/ Biscuits

1 - #You can turn into a powdery being of some kind (like sentient snow, carnivorous alien death spores, nanites, etc.). If you wish, this can be your permanent form.

2 - You can spin inhumanly fast, allowing you to travel over surfaces at a high rate of speed and inflict superhuman damage.

3 - #You're some kind of robot. Boost three of your attributes to superhuman capacity.

4 - You've got a weapon of mass destruction: something with an effect that's beyond superhuman. Does it have to be lethal? No. Just know that it's overwhelmingly powerful. Feel free to mix other power(s) with it, then set the details.

5 - If you consume metal while injured, you'll heal by the second.

Recipe #230 – Combat Gymnast Gelatin

1 - #You're an athlete with peak human (maybe even superhuman) skill. What's your sport?

2 - You can dodge almost any attack you see coming. It's the "un-dodgeable" attacks that you have to worry about (like a bullet to the back, an oncoming avalanche, etc.).

3 - You have some kind of kinetic beam attack. No, it doesn't do heat or explosive damage. It just pokes a hole through whatever it can penetrate.

4 - While you do need to sleep, you'll never become exhausted from sustained physical or mental activity.

5 - Close your eyes and you'll be able to "see" in all directions at the same time. Naturally, you can function/fight/read better this way. Set the details for this power.

Recipe #231 – Country-friend Bandit

1 - #You are—or were—a professional villain. Pick up a criminal skill specialty that you can utilize, with superhuman capacity.

2 - You have an extensive network of reliable criminal contacts.

3 - You have a useful network of mystical contacts.

4 - You have the loyalty of a very dangerous being. Assign this individual three powers and a backstory.

5 - You always find whatever you need to achieve your objective(s). Too bad having the right tools doesn't guarantee success.

Recipe #232 – Creamed Alchemical Monstrosity

1 - Think of your tongue as an extendable weapon. The range, damage type(s), and other details are up to you.

2 - Your skin's hardened against both physical and mystical attacks.

3 - You can convert other beings into whatever you are (and pass along powers, skills, weaknesses, etc.). Anyone you train/turn is inclined to obey you.

4 - Somehow, you can spray a fast-acting corrosive. Set the details (range, potency, etc.).

5 - #Whatever you are, you can't pass for a human. Boost two of your human-scale attributes to superhuman capacity. Set the details on what kind of creature you are.

Recipe #233 – Crème-filled Enchanter

    1 - #You can enchant objects—both temporarily and permanently.

    2 - You can create regular (or customized) archaic melee weapons out of thin air. Feel free to merge other powers with this one.

    3 - You're almost immune to all of your other powers (should they ever be used on you or somehow misfire).

    4 - You can undo the effect(s) of one of your other powers—unless it's too late.

    5 - Normally, it takes two actions to draw a weapon and then use it. Well, you're so fast that you can make it count as one action. If feasible, this advantage can also be applied to another power(s).

Recipe #234 – Crisis Symbiote Cookie Bars

1 - #You can cast spells. How that works is up to you. Boost your Will attribute to superhuman capacity.

2 - #You're cursed to stumble into constant dangers that you must never avoid (or you will suffer).

3 - #You're a world-class expert in the occult, with secrets worth killing for.

4 - #For every serious flaw you give yourself, you can pick up one free power.

5 - #You have some kind of symbiote within your body (biological, psychic, tech-based, mystical, etc.). Feel free to merge your other power(s) with it.

Recipe #235 – Crunchy Flinger

1 - #Whether you're a genius or just pretty quick-witted, you often make very good decisions—to the point where people tend to follow you.

2 - You can throw non-weapon objects with a skill beyond superhuman. Whatever you can lift is fair game—from baseballs to lamps to crowded buses.

3 - You can touch an object, charge it with psychic energy, then make it explode on impact.

4 - Normally, it takes two actions to draw a weapon and then use it. Well, you're so fast that you can make it count as one action. If feasible, this advantage can also be applied to another power(s).

5 - Your distance attacks will harmlessly pass through the first solid object they hit (like a wall or body armor), then turn solid again. Set the details.

Recipe #236 – Cursed Denture Sundae

1 - #You're old, wise, and can move like a prime athlete.

2 - Until they see you in action, people tend to ignore and underestimate you.

3 - You have a subtle way to make someone suicidal, at superhuman capacity.

4 - You can make a sacrificial offering to a higher being, in exchange for whatever you want. The bigger the "ask," the bigger your offering has to be—from favors to wealth to victims. Set the details. Feel free to merge another power(s) with this one.

5 - You've got an indestructible (mystical) item/weapon that'll return to you from anywhere. When wielding it, any feats you make are in the superhuman range. Any powers you merge with it will go beyond superhuman capacity.

Recipe #237 – Cursed Mime Pizzelle

1 - If you don't say a word, it throws off your opponents—whether you're playing poker or fighting to the death. The longer you maintain this silence, the more mistakes your target(s) make.

2 - #You are—or were—a professional villain. Pick up a criminal skill specialty that you can utilize, with superhuman capacity.

3 - #You've mastered a non-mystical fighting style, which allows you to fight with superhuman capacity.

4 - You can convert other beings into whatever you are (and pass along powers, skills, weaknesses, etc.). Anyone you train/turn is inclined to obey you.

5 - You have access to a loyal group of combat-hardened minions. Give them gear and an origin story (hired mercs, temporary conjurations, members of your tribe, etc.).

Recipe #238 – Cyberdemon Enchiladas

1 - #You're a cyborg, to the point where most of your body's been replaced with artificial components. Feel free to mix your other powers into this one. Are any of your attributes increased?

2 - #You've got demonic blood in you. Pick up one extra power and boost two of your attributes to superhuman. Now, what kind of demon are you?

3 - You have a number of lesser powers, which must be inspired by one of your other abilities.

4 - Your weapons, implants, and/or gear have safeguards against theft, sabotage, etc.

5 - You can safely cross into other dimensions. Doesn't mean you'll make it back though . . .

Recipe #239 – Dairy Free Tribal Kid

1 - You can hide or sneak about with a skill that's beyond superhuman. That makes you among the stealthiest bastards alive.

2 - #Your skills at wilderness combat, survival, and tracking are at superhuman capacity.

3 - As long as you're moving around, incoming attacks tend to miss you. This power works at superhuman capacity—even on attacks you don't see coming. Of course, some attacks can't be dodged.

4 - #You're a remarkable kid. How is up to you. Pick one attribute and boost it to superhuman capacity.

5 - You always find whatever you need to achieve your objective(s). Too bad having the right tools doesn't guarantee success.

Recipe #240 – Dam Pokhtak Prison Blade

1 - Your weapons, implants, and/or gear have safeguards against theft, sabotage, etc.

2 - You have a number of lesser powers, which must be inspired by one of your other abilities.

3 - You've got an indestructible (mystical) item/weapon that'll return to you from anywhere. When wielding it, any feats you make are in the superhuman range. Any powers you merge with it will go beyond superhuman capacity.

4 - You can phase beings into yourself and lock them into a sort of stasis. During this time, you can access their powers, attributes, and memories. Set the limitations for this ability.

5 - You have a useful, chatty object (like an implant, ship's AI, or talking mage's staff). Feel free to merge your other (relevant) powers with it.

Recipe #241 – Death Chef Fingers

1 - Your grip inflicts superhuman force (even if you're not super-strong). How'd you acquire this ability?

2 - You can create solid, non-living, organic matter (no weapons!) out of thin air—from fresh herbs to raw meat.

3 - Your skill with a knife is beyond superhuman. The things you can do with one are epic . . .

4 - Your grappling skills (offensive and defensive) are beyond superhuman. Only a special few can match you.

5 - You can poison any organic food with only a touch.

Recipe #242 – Death's Rogue Minion w/ Clams

1 - #You've mastered a mystical fighting style. That's why your fighting and acrobatic abilities are at superhuman capacity, along with your striking damage.

2 - Nothing scares you. Period.

3 - #You can cast spells. How that works is up to you. Boost your Will attribute to superhuman capacity.

4 - #You're a powerful minion (with perks and flaws) who answers to Death. Pick up two extra powers that will help with your duties.

5 - If killed in the presence of mystical evil, you'll quickly self-resurrect.

Recipe #243 – Debt Collector Skewers

1 - You have an unarmed fighting skill that's beyond superhuman.

2 - Your touch can inflict shock damage.

3 - Your touch can reduce a target's innate powers to virtually nothing for several minutes.

4 - #You can intimidate people with a superhuman capacity. When you get "scary," those with weaker minds might actually run away from you.

5 - #You're a genetic superhuman (born or augmented) with one free power and one superhuman attribute.

Recipe #244 – Defective Speedster Rolls

1 - #You're a speedster, which allows you to move at superhuman capacity (and probably faster than sound).

2 - #For every serious flaw you give yourself, you can pick up one free power.

3 - You have a form-fitting mundane forcefield, which offers you protection beyond superhuman capacity. Feel free to merge this power with other (relevant) ones.

4 - Focus on a target and you'll instinctively guess three absolutely correct things about him/her/it.

5 - You never have to sleep.

Recipe #245 – Defensive Wall Nuggets

1 - Stomp on a flat surface and some kind of barrier wall appears. What's it made of?

2 - If a solid object hits you (like a punch or a speeding truck), this power will reflect the kinetic energy toward its exact point of origin. Do sharp objects count?

3 - Find enough natural ground and you can make it wrap around you (as a form-fitting armor), with three of your attributes boosted to superhuman capacity.

4 - You can sense the presence of threats and their general location(s).

5 - You can reflect a mystical attack right back to its source—even if it's beyond superhuman capacity. Does this also apply to benign magicks?

Recipe #246 – Deli Style Boxer

1 - The pain of others can heal you (by the second). Just inflict the pain or hang out near agonized beings.

2 - #You're an athlete with peak human (maybe even superhuman) skill. What's your sport?

3 - If in a fight, focus on one target (at a time) and you'll be able to correctly anticipate that foe's every move.

4 - Whenever you make a melee-ranged strike, any armor or barrier in your way will briefly phase. Thus, you could stab someone through a suit of armor (like it wasn't there) and kill its wearer.

5 - With this ability, you can take enough of a pounding to kill you three times over.

Recipe #247 – Demon Gardener Baklava

1 - You can control and alter the genetic structure of any living vegetation you look upon. Set the details.

2 - From miles out, you can establish two-way telepathic contact with a handful of minds. Feel free to merge this power with other relevant abilities.

3 - #You're a plant-based lifeform and cannot pass for human.

4 - Any offspring you have will grow to full maturity within a matter of hours. Set the details on how this happens (alien DNA, magic, genetic flaw, etc.).

5 - #You've got demonic blood in you. Pick up one extra power and boost two of your attributes to superhuman. Now, what kind of demon are you?

Recipe #248 – Demonic Asylum Cabbage

1 - You can safely cross into other dimensions. Doesn't mean you'll make it back though . . .

2 - You have your very own pocket dimension. Assign the rules, perks, and drawbacks to such a place.

3 - When you die, any of your innate powers and mystical items will automatically go to a pre-designated heir(s).

4 - #You can cast spells. How that works is up to you. Boost your Will attribute to superhuman capacity.

5 - Someone (or something) is obligated to watch your back. This could be a bodyguard, demon familiar, loyal AI, etc.

Recipe #249 – Dipped Threat Suit

1 - Your costume and/or uniform counts as lightweight body armor. Feel free to mix this power with any others you might have.

2 - You have a useful, chatty object (like an implant, ship's AI, or talking mage's staff). Feel free to merge your other (relevant) powers with it.

3 - You have a number of lesser powers, which must be inspired by one of your other abilities.

4 - Any tech you make/own/use can (to a point) self-repair.

5 - Your weapons, implants, and/or gear have safeguards against theft, sabotage, etc.

Recipe #250 – Dragon Archaeologist Pesto

1 - #You have a superhuman mastery of one non-mystical skill set (from doctor to pianist to CEO).

2 - #You have a superhuman flair for finding people and solving mysteries—whether you're a spy, lawman, freelance sleuth, or someone's pet enforcer.

3 - #You're a world-class expert in the occult, with secrets worth killing for.

4 - #You're a full-blooded dragon. Aside from the wings, enhanced attributes, armored scales, and a breath attack, add the little perks and flaws.

5 - #You can copy the appearance and voices of other humanoid beings.

Recipe #251 – Dream Cultist Salad

1 - You can enter and control the dreams of others.

2 - You have access to a toxin that renders most targets unconscious upon contact. Duration and after-effects are up to you.

3 - #You're a well-versed killer. Your talents can be merely human or at superhuman capacity.

4 - You can make a sacrificial offering to a higher being, in exchange for whatever you want. The bigger the "ask," the bigger your offering has to be—from favors to wealth to victims. Set the details. Feel free to merge another power(s) with this one.

5 - You can indefinitely alter a target's entire worldview, with superhuman capacity.

Recipe #252 – Dream Knight Kale

1 - #You have an overwhelming need to do good—even if you're a benign crook. Boost two of your attributes to superhuman capacity.

2 - You can make intangible spirits and mystical entities solid—either as a favor or to better fight them. Is this a temporary effect? Can you use this power on yourself? Set the details.

3 - You have a number of lesser powers, which must be inspired by one of your other abilities.

4 - You know how to do exorcisms (whether by ritual magic, a mystical object, innate power, or some other means).

5 - You can enter and control the dreams of others.

Recipe #253 – Drone Sniper Cheeseburgers

1 - Your costume and/or uniform counts as lightweight body armor. Feel free to mix this power with any others you might have.

2 - Your sniper skills are beyond superhuman.

3 - You have a projectile weapon that fires sensor-filled ammo.

4 - If you wish, technological devices can't detect you—from cameras to high-end sensors.

5 - You can control/remote-pilot your weapons, constructs, and gadgetry from far away—with superhuman skill.

Recipe #254 – Drunken Sniper Beets

1 - If you aim for only a few seconds, you tend to make incredibly difficult shots (either from range or even on the move).

2 - You can make a distance attack that can hit multiple targets, either at once or in very rapid succession.

3 - #You have extensive military experience and a natural affinity with any kind of weapon. Also, boost one of your attributes to superhuman capacity.

4 - #Each type (or even brand) of alcohol will give you a different, temporary power.

5 - You have a high-powered firearm of some kind, which does superhuman damage.

Recipe #255 – Dystopian Competitor
Pomegranate

1 - #You're an athlete with peak human (maybe even superhuman) skill. What's your sport?

2 - Whenever you're in a dangerous situation, you'll have unnaturally good luck—until the crisis ends. Then your luck returns to normal.

3 - Nothing scares you. Period.

4 - During a fight, you'll be able to ignore your injuries (from broken bones to fatal wounds) until the fight's over—then it'll all catch up to you. Note: certain injuries will still kill you on the spot (like decapitation or a nuke blast).

5 - #You're a super genius with several non-violent skill masteries (set the details). Boost your Intellect to superhuman capacity.

Recipe #256 – Earth Merc Fish Sticks

1 - You can look at an object and know its structural status (including weak spots).

2 - You can start earthquakes and maintain them for as long as you concentrate.

3 - Find enough natural ground and you can make it wrap around you (as a form-fitting armor), with three of your attributes boosted to superhuman capacity.

4 - The proximity of natural ground allows you to regenerate (from most injuries) by the second.

5 - You can tunnel through solid surfaces.

Recipe #257 – Elven Pirate Massaman

1 - You have access to a loyal group of combat-hardened minions. Give them gear and an origin story (hired mercs, temporary conjurations, members of your tribe, etc.).

2 - You have a unique, feature-loaded vehicle (from a spy car to an attack sub to a star cruiser).

3 - #You can just "snap" and plow into fights with a merciless rage and (temporarily) boosted Intellect. Do any other attributes increase to superhuman capacity? Will you only attack enemies, while enraged?

4 - #You have enough elven blood to get the perks (attributes, longevity, etc.).

5 - #Whether you're a genius or just pretty quick-witted, you often make very good decisions—to the point where people tend to follow you.

Recipe #258 – Empath Killer T-bone

1 - #You're a well-versed killer. Your talents can be merely human or at superhuman capacity.

2 - You can indefinitely alter a target's entire worldview, with superhuman capacity.

3 - Pick one of your other powers and permanently amplify it beyond superhuman capacity.

4 - A superhuman-capacity defense protects your mind against psychic attacks.

5 - You can establish two-way psychic contact with up to hundreds of minds (maybe more), within a one-mile range.

Recipe #259 – Enslaver's Yogurt

1 - #You're playfully insane—until angered. Also, your mind's immune to mental intrusions of any kind. Boost your Endurance, Will, or Intellect to superhuman capacity.

2 - Somehow, you can view a target (surroundings and all) from up to a certain range. Is this astral projection, magic, or something else? If relevant, you can mix this power with other abilities.

3 - You can control a living target's body, like one would a puppet.

4 - You can automatically track a number of targets anywhere on the globe.

5 - #You're part of a hive mind. Set the details. Feel free to merge another relevant power(s) with this one.

Recipe #260 – Exploding Swords Soft Wrap

1 - With a touch, you can "program" an inanimate object to explode under a particular set of circumstances.

2 - You can create regular (or customized) archaic melee weapons out of thin air. Feel free to merge other powers with this one.

3 - You can pick up an object and see its past.

4 - Merge this ability with any area-effect power/weapon you have. When using it, you can spare anyone or anything within its range (but nail everyone else). For this power to work, do you have to know where your "friendlies" are first?

5 - Your skill with a sword's beyond superhuman.

Recipe #261 – Face Thief Chicken

1 - #You've got demonic blood in you. Pick up one extra power and boost two of your attributes to superhuman. Now, what kind of demon are you?

2 - Put on someone's face and you can (indefinitely) become that person.

3 - You've got a (possibly useful) tail on your body—or maybe you slither around/swim with one.

4 - You can safely cross into other dimensions. Doesn't mean you'll make it back though . . .

5 - The souls of your victims end up your loyal slaves. Lay out the perks and limitations of this macabre ability.

Recipe #262 – Falafel Scout

1 - #You have extensive military experience and a natural affinity with any kind of weapon. Also, boost one of your attributes to superhuman capacity.

2 - From miles out, you can establish two-way telepathic contact with a handful of minds. Feel free to merge this power with other relevant abilities.

3 - Focus on a target and you'll instinctively guess three absolutely correct things about him/her/it.

4 - You can teleport (with one passenger) across a certain range.

5 - You can turn invisible to all forms of detection (the five senses, psychics, tech, and even magic). Set the details and limitations.

Recipe #263 – Fearless Idiot w/ Dill Sauce

1 - #You're incurably stupid BUT one of your other powers is boosted far beyond superhuman capacity.

2 - Nothing scares you. Period.

3 - In your hands, any mundane weapon inflicts superhuman mystical damage. The effect ends right after you let the weapon go.

4 - #You're cursed to stumble into constant dangers that you must never avoid (or you will suffer).

5 - Whenever you're in a dangerous situation, you'll have unnaturally good luck—until the crisis ends. Then your luck returns to normal.

Recipe #264 – Flamenco Killer Mac & Cheese

1 - You kick with a skill that's beyond superhuman.

2 - If in a fight, focus on one target (at a time) and you'll be able to correctly anticipate that foe's every move.

3 - A single blow to a living target (in armed or unarmed combat) should be considered a death blow. Even a punch to the jaw might count.

4 - You're very adept at striking multiple targets, via melee attacks, practically at the same time. How does that work?

5 - You can leap up, down, and across great distances. Yeah, your kicking strength's superhuman.

Recipe #265 – Fortune-teller Lentil

1 - #You have accurate visions of the future. Set the details and limitations.

2 - You can bless people with random good luck, which lasts for days at a time.

3 - You can inflict bursts of bad luck, which might range from annoying to deadly. The type and duration of misfortunes are unpredictable.

4 - You can convert other beings into whatever you are (and pass along powers, skills, weaknesses, etc.). Anyone you train/turn is inclined to obey you.

5 - #You've mastered a non-mystical fighting style, which allows you to fight with superhuman capacity.

Recipe #266 – Fruit Salad Healer

1 - #You're a remarkable kid. How is up to you. Pick one attribute and boost it to superhuman capacity.

2 - You can sing to one person (even yourself) and undo injuries/illnesses within a few minutes.

3 - Via some form of contact, you can free someone else's mind from external influence (assuming your power's strong enough).

4 - You can bring back the dead.

5 - Once per day, you can cure any mystical curse/infection/ailment with a touch—even your own.

Recipe #267 – Fudge Speed Thief

1 - Your battle armor protects you from damage and raises your Might attribute to superhuman capacity. What other features does it have? Feel free to merge another power(s) with this one.

2 - #You're a speedster, which allows you to move at superhuman capacity (and probably faster than sound).

3 - You have some kind of sensor tech that functions at superhuman capacity.

4 - You can heal from most injuries within a few minutes.

5 - You can do hundreds of small actions per second (from trigger pulls to punches to fast-building something). What are the limitations?

Recipe #268 – Future Demon Bolognese

1 - #You've got demonic blood in you. Pick up one extra power and boost two of your attributes to superhuman. Now, what kind of demon are you?

2 - You can travel into the past and safely return. Set the details, ranges, and drawbacks.

3 - You can persuade folks to do things your way with superhuman capacity.

4 - You can use weapons with a skill that's beyond superhuman. Feel free to merge another power(s) with this one.

5 - #Somehow, information flows to you (from financial data to military secrets to occult mysteries to stuff no human should ever know). Set the details, origins, and any downsides.

Recipe #269 – Geno-skeletal Sashimi

1 - You have a hardened skeleton, which is useful in a crash or a fistfight.

2 - You can shoot razor-sharp shards. What (one) material are they made of? Feel free to mix this power with any others you might have.

3 - You've got a (possibly useful) tail on your body—or maybe you slither around/swim with one.

4 - You can make spikes PAINFULLY sprout from someone else's body. How does that work?

5 - #Whatever you are, you can't pass for a human. Boost two of your human-scale attributes to superhuman capacity. Set the details on what kind of creature you are.

Recipe #270 – Getaway Driver Meringue

1 - Your skill's beyond superhuman when driving or flying a vehicle—even for the first time.

2 - You have an extensive network of reliable criminal contacts.

3 - You always find whatever you need to achieve your objective(s). Too bad having the right tools doesn't guarantee success.

4 - If you selfishly retreat from a threat (without regard for anyone else), you'll always escape.

5 - You have a unique, feature-loaded vehicle (from a spy car to an attack sub to a star cruiser).

Recipe #271 – Ghost Ship Couscous

1 - You have a unique, feature-loaded vehicle (from a spy car to an attack sub to a star cruiser).

2 - If you immerse yourself in water, you can teleport to a watery location that's closest to your intended destination (like an ocean, pond, swimming pool, or even a filled bathtub).

3 - You can create a dense, instant, and area-effect fog around yourself. Yeah, you can see through it just fine. Feel free to mix this with other (relevant) powers.

4 - You have a useful, chatty object (like an implant, ship's AI, or talking mage's staff). Feel free to merge your other (relevant) powers with it.

5 - You have access to a loyal group of combat-hardened minions. Give them gear and an origin story (hired mercs, temporary conjurations, members of your tribe, etc.).

Recipe #272 – Grab Team Sauerbraten

1 - You can teleport alone or with a small group of beings.

2 - #You have extensive military experience and a natural affinity with any kind of weapon. Also, boost one of your attributes to superhuman capacity.

3 - You have a small arsenal of offensive and/or defensive gadgetry.

4 - You have access to a loyal group of combat-hardened minions. Give them gear and an origin story (hired mercs, temporary conjurations, members of your tribe, etc.).

5 - You have a non-lethal energy attack that will stun humans and most superhumans.

Recipe #273 – Grizzled Ice Wielder Muesli

1 - You can emit a beam that inflicts superhuman cold damage and encases whatever it hits in solid ice. Feel free to merge another power(s) with this one.

2 - Somehow, you can make liquids move (pretty much) however you want them to.

3 - If placed in sub-zero temperatures, you'll regenerate by the minute.

4 - In a sub-zero environment, your Speed, Endurance, Might, and Health attributes all become superhuman. Once removed from it, those attributes will return to normal.

5 - #Your skills at wilderness combat, survival, and tracking are at superhuman capacity.

Recipe #274 – Half-alien w/ Sprinkles

1 - #You have alien blood in your veins. Boost two of your attributes to superhuman capacity.

2 - #You can temporarily grow a bit taller and sprout extra muscles. Boost your Speed, Endurance, Might, and Health attributes to superhuman capacity. Set the details (including duration) and feel free to merge another power(s) with this one.

3 - Your skin self-hardens (like armor) just before anything harmful can hit you.

4 - You have an extensive network of extraterrestrial contacts.

5 - You have a focused beam attack that puts molten holes through most targets, with superhuman capacity.

Recipe #275 – Half-elven Hitman Greens

1 - #You have enough elven blood to get the perks (attributes, longevity, etc.).

2 - #You're a well-versed killer. Your talents can be merely human or at superhuman capacity.

3 - #For every serious flaw you give yourself, you can pick up one free power.

4 - You can heal from most injuries within a few minutes.

5 - You've got an indestructible (mystical) item/weapon that'll return to you from anywhere. When wielding it, any feats you make are in the superhuman range. Any powers you merge with it will go beyond superhuman capacity.

Recipe #276 – Homemade Ninja Thief

1 - #You've mastered a non-mystical fighting style, which allows you to fight with superhuman capacity.

2 - Your skill at bypassing security measures is beyond superhuman capacity.

3 - Establish eye contact and you can hypnotize a target(s) at superhuman capacity.

4 - You have a one-of-a-kind, non-mystical weapon. You can wield it with superhuman skill. Its material strength is beyond superhuman capacity. Set the other details.

5 - You have a small arsenal of offensive and/or defensive gadgetry.

Recipe #277 – Honey Chipotle Weremobster

1 - You have access to a loyal group of combat-hardened minions. Give them gear and an origin story (hired mercs, temporary conjurations, members of your tribe, etc.).

2 - #You're a lycanthrope, with the appropriate perks and limitations. Pick a sub-breed (werewolf, weretiger, werebat, etc.).

3 - #You are—or were—a professional villain. Pick up a criminal skill specialty that you can utilize, with superhuman capacity.

4 - You answer to someone (or something) with a lot of useful connections and influence. This individual can ease your path, save your life, or have you killed for too many failures.

5 - You can convert other beings into whatever you are (and pass along powers, skills, weaknesses, etc.). Anyone you train/turn is inclined to obey you.

Recipe #278 – Hosin Pork w/ Drug Witch

1 - You have a chemistry skill that's beyond superhuman capacity.

2 - #You can cast spells. How that works is up to you. Boost your Will attribute to superhuman capacity.

3 - You have access to an addictive drug. Set the details and feel free to merge them with other powers.

4 - #You're an alchemist with a finite number of potion formulas in your head. While they take time and materials to brew up, each potion's a temporary "power in a bottle." Set the perks and limitations.

5 - You have an extensive network of reliable criminal contacts.

Recipe #279 – Hot-smoked Scoundrel

1 - #You are stunningly attractive and/or charismatic, which allows you to convince people to do whatever you want (at superhuman capacity).

2 - #Somehow, you're very wealthy (probably with billions to your name).

3 - You have an unarmed fighting skill that's beyond superhuman.

4 - #You can't feel emotions of any kind. Boost either your Intellect or Will attribute to superhuman capacity.

5 - Your skill with a sword's beyond superhuman.

Recipe #280 – Ice Monster Toast

1 - Your hair/fur is armored and will protect whatever it covers.

2 - #Whatever you are, you can't pass for a human. Boost two of your human-scale attributes to superhuman capacity. Set the details on what kind of creature you are.

3 - You have a painful, paralytic bite.

4 - You can track a target (by scent alone) from miles away.

5 - You've got some kind of edged attack that's a part of you (claws, horns, fangs, etc.).

Recipe #281 – Illusion Master Spatzle

1 - You can establish two-way psychic contact with up to hundreds of minds (maybe more), within a one-mile range.

2 - You can make beings experience illusions (across all five senses), at superhuman capacity.

3 - Pick one of your other powers and permanently amplify it beyond superhuman capacity.

4 - When merged with this ability, certain powers (like telekinesis) can stay active for a while longer—even after an interruption of some kind (like lost concentration or contact). Hopefully, this will buy you enough time to re-establish the ability or beat a hasty retreat. Set the duration.

5 - You can read and/or copy a target's memories, at superhuman capacity.

Recipe #282 – Illusionist Bundt Cake

1 - You can make one of your other powers' (temporary) effects permanent.

2 - You can get rid of one weakness/limitation within one of your other powers. However, you must replace it with a "replacement weakness/limitation" of some kind (your choice).*

3 - You can create audio-visual holographic illusions.

4 - #You can temporarily bring images of objects (but not living beings) to life.*

5 - Anyone you sire, "turn," or conjure into existence can only be harmed, destroyed, or killed by magic.

Recipe #283 – Implanted Cop w/ Wild Rice

1 - You have hundreds of skills in your head (maybe more).

2 - You have an extensive network of reliable criminal contacts.

3 - #You have some kind of symbiote within your body (biological, psychic, tech-based, mystical, etc.). Feel free to merge your other power(s) with it.

4 - You have a small arsenal of offensive and/or defensive gadgetry.

5 - You have a high-powered firearm of some kind, which does superhuman damage.

Recipe #284 – Infectious Hive T-bone

1 - You answer to someone (or something) with a lot of useful connections and influence. This individual can ease your path, save your life, or have you killed for too many failures.

2 - You can convert other beings into whatever you are (and pass along powers, skills, weaknesses, etc.). Anyone you train/turn is inclined to obey you.

3 - #You're a genetic superhuman (born or augmented) with one free power and one superhuman attribute.

4 - As long as you're working/fighting alongside allies, your side will always beat the odds. Why?

5 - #You're part of a hive mind. Set the details. Feel free to merge another relevant power(s) with this one.

Recipe #285 – Invisible Gunslinger Shrimp

1 - As long as you're moving around, incoming attacks tend to miss you. This power works at superhuman capacity—even on attacks you don't see coming. Of course, some attacks can't be dodged.

2 - You can turn invisible to all forms of detection (the five senses, psychics, tech, and even magic). Set the details and limitations.

3 - You always find whatever you need to achieve your objective(s). Too bad having the right tools doesn't guarantee success.

4 - Your skill with pistols is beyond superhuman capacity.

5 - For better or worse, your name is feared far and wide. Set the pros and cons of having such an infamous rep.

Recipe #286 – Jellied Coven Mistress

1 - You can convert other beings into whatever you are (and pass along powers, skills, weaknesses, etc.). Anyone you train/turn is inclined to obey you.

2 - You can undo the effect(s) of one of your other powers—unless it's too late.

3 - Bad things happen to those who break an agreement with you. Feel free to mix another power(s) with this one.

4 - #You can cast spells. How that works is up to you. Boost your Will attribute to superhuman capacity.

5 - You can borrow a power from one of your offspring/minions (if applicable).

Recipe #287 – Jinxed Cop Okra

1 - #You have a superhuman flair for finding people and solving mysteries—whether you're a spy, lawman, freelance sleuth, or someone's pet enforcer.

2 - Focus on a target and you'll instinctively guess three absolutely correct things about him/her/it.

3 - You automatically sense when other people (within a certain range) are in danger, including enough details to interfere—if you want to.

4 - #You're cursed to stumble into constant dangers that you must never avoid (or you will suffer).

5 - You always find whatever you need to achieve your objective(s). Too bad having the right tools doesn't guarantee success.

Recipe #288 – Kinetic Boxer Snaps

1 - Any unarmed blow you make will inflict beyond superhuman damage—even if your strength's merely human.

2 - Your skin's hardened against both physical and mundane energy attacks.

3 - You have a hardened skeleton, which is useful in a crash or a fistfight.

4 - #You're an athlete with peak human (maybe even superhuman) skill. What's your sport?

5 - Your punching skills are beyond superhuman capacity.

Recipe #289 – Kisscurser Velouté

1 - Your kiss can (temporarily) make almost anyone fall in love with you.

2 - You've mastered a number of potent curse enchantments that can be inflicted upon your targets.

3 - Until they see you in action, people tend to ignore and underestimate you.

4 - You can use another power on a target and delay its effect(s).

5 - #You've mastered a non-mystical fighting style, which allows you to fight with superhuman capacity.

Recipe #290 – Last Heir Nuggets

1 - #You're a remarkable kid. How is up to you. Pick one attribute and boost it to superhuman capacity.

2 - You have a number of lesser powers, which must be inspired by one of your other abilities.

3 - Someone (or something) is obligated to watch your back. This could be a bodyguard, demon familiar, loyal AI, etc.

4 - #Somehow, you're very wealthy (probably with billions to your name).

5 - Your battle armor protects you from damage and raises your Might attribute to superhuman capacity. What other features does it have? Feel free to merge another power(s) with this one.

Recipe #291 – Lemon Butter Dream Monk

1 - You can enter and control the dreams of others.

2 - You can trap your victims within their own minds. The comatose effect's indefinite and can't be undone by modern medicine. Feel free to merge another power(s) with this one.

3 - #You've mastered a mystical fighting style. That's why your fighting and acrobatic abilities are at superhuman capacity, along with your striking damage.

4 - If you can establish psychic contact, this power will let you feed on a target's mind without having to be in the room. Whether it's for sustenance, to recover lost Health, or both is up to you.

5 - You can control a living target's body, like one would a puppet.

Recipe #292 – Liquid Gadget Cordon Bleu

1 - #You can turn into a living mass of liquid. If you wish this to be your permanent state, that's fine too.

2 - You can turn parts of your body into small devices. Set the details and limitations. Feel free to merge another power(s) with this one.

3 - You can turn parts of your body into whatever small weaponry you wish. Set the details and limitations. Feel free to merge this ability with any other relevant power(s).

4 - Lose an appendage and it can move on its own and reattach with ease. If it's utterly destroyed, it won't regenerate.

5 - If injured, you can regain Health by consuming safe liquids.

Recipe #293 – Magslinger & Fennel Slaw

1 - You can generate magnetic energy fields and use them to move ferrous objects. Set the details. Feel free to merge this ability with other relevant powers.

2 - Normally, it takes two actions to draw a weapon and then use it. Well, you're so fast that you can make it count as one action. If feasible, this advantage can also be applied to another power(s).

3 - You can fly. Set the details and feel free to merge another power(s) with this one.

4 - You can automatically detect and identify the presence of any natural minerals within your power's range.

5 - You have a high-powered firearm of some kind, which does superhuman damage.

Recipe #294 – Mastermind Noodles

1 - #Whether you're a genius or just pretty quick-witted, you often make very good decisions—to the point where people tend to follow you.

2 - You have hundreds of skills in your head (maybe more).

3 - You have a number of lesser powers, which must be inspired by one of your other abilities.

4 - #You are—or were—a professional villain. Pick up a criminal skill specialty that you can utilize, with superhuman capacity.

5 - You've got a secret lair, with sufficient resources to pursue your objectives (whatever they may be).

Recipe #295 – Matchmaker Salsa

1 - You can make one of your other powers' (temporary) effects permanent.

2 - You can temporarily make someone love anyone/anything (except for you).

3 - Focus on a target and you'll instinctively guess three absolutely correct things about him/her/it.

4 - You can undo the effect(s) of one of your other powers—unless it's too late.

5 - #You're a well-versed killer. Your talents can be merely human or at superhuman capacity.

Recipe #296 – Merc Medic Pizzadillas

1 - You have a secret lab with the resources to pursue your objectives.

2 - You have a unique, feature-loaded vehicle (from a spy car to an attack sub to a star cruiser).

3 - Your battle armor protects you from damage and raises your Might attribute to superhuman capacity. What other features does it have? Feel free to merge another power(s) with this one.

4 - You have a small arsenal of offensive and/or defensive gadgetry.

5 - You have access to a loyal group of combat-hardened minions. Give them gear and an origin story (hired mercs, temporary conjurations, members of your tribe, etc.).

Recipe #297 – Mind Drinker Caviar

1 - #You're a world-class expert in the occult, with secrets worth killing for.

2 - You can temporarily paralyze someone, via touch.

3 - Establish contact and you can "drink" your victims' memories and skills away by the second.

4 - You have a weapon that resembles a harmless object (like a guitar blaster or sword cane).

5 - #You're old, wise, and can move like a prime athlete.

Recipe #298 – Minestrone Sound Monster

1 - You can create a zone of pure silence around you. Set the details—including which powers this ability might reduce or cancel out.

2 - You can jam various signals (like sensors or communications) with a range of X miles.

3 - #Whatever you are, you can't pass for a human. Boost two of your human-scale attributes to superhuman capacity. Set the details on what kind of creature you are.

4 - You have a noticeable organic armor that's permanently bonded to you (like a shell).

5 - #You're a truly evil monster who must feed upon the living to survive. Boost two of your human-scale attributes to superhuman capacity.

Recipe #299 – Mini Lemon Mindsmasher

1 - #You have enough telepathic DNA to read surface thoughts (at superhuman capacity). Replace one of your other powers with something psychic—if you want to.

2 - X number of times per day, you can generate a massive psychic shockwave in all directions. Feel free to mix other powers with this one. Overusing this power might fry your mind or just kill you.

3 - You know the precise location of every living thing around you.

4 - Merge this ability with any area-effect power/weapon you have. When using it, you can spare anyone or anything within its range (but nail everyone else). For this power to work, do you have to know where your "friendlies" are first?

5 - You can inflict total and permanent memory loss, with superhuman capacity. If you're feeling nice, you might leave a few "crumbs" behind.

Recipe #300 – Mob Hacker Fajitas

1 - #You are—or were—a professional villain. Pick up a criminal skill specialty that you can utilize, with superhuman capacity.

2 - Your skill with computers (both hardware and software) is beyond superhuman.

3 - You have an extensive network of reliable criminal contacts.

4 - You have access to a reliable network of allies within business, government, and other legitimate sectors of society.

5 - You have easy access to a vast amount of previously stored information (what kind is up to you).

Recipe #301 – Molecular Quinoa

1 - #You're a genetic superhuman (born or augmented) with one free power and one superhuman attribute.

2 - #With a touch, you can turn an inanimate object into something else. Set the limitations for this power.

3 - You can turn living victims into inanimate objects.

4 - #You're a super genius with several non-violent skill masteries (set the details). Boost your Intellect to superhuman capacity.

5 - Normally, it takes two actions to draw a weapon and then use it. Well, you're so fast that you can make it count as one action. If feasible, this advantage can also be applied to another power(s).

Recipe #302 – Monkey Fighter Potatoes

1 - #Whatever you are, you can't pass for a human. Boost two of your human-scale attributes to superhuman capacity. Set the details on what kind of creature you are.

2 - You've got a (possibly useful) tail on your body—or maybe you slither around/swim with one.

3 - #You've mastered a non-mystical fighting style, which allows you to fight with superhuman capacity.

4 - If your melee strikes hit a human and pain is inflicted, then he/she will automatically fall unconscious. Only those with certain armors and/or defensive powers (like an increased Endurance attribute) can withstand this attack.

5 - Your hair/fur is armored and will protect whatever it covers.

Recipe #303 – Monster Hunter Eggplant

1 - #You have a superhuman flair for finding people and solving mysteries—whether you're a spy, lawman, freelance sleuth, or someone's pet enforcer.

2 - If you have the means to investigate (and a day's time), you can determine a target's weakness(es).

3 - You'll automatically know if someone's lying to you.

4 - #You're meaner than most people. Boost your Endurance and Will attributes to superhuman capacity.

5 - You can automatically detect the presence of magic, within a certain range.

Recipe #304 – Monster-slaying Prostitute Fondue

1 - #You are stunningly attractive and/or charismatic, which allows you to convince people to do whatever you want (at superhuman capacity).

2 - #You have extensive military experience and a natural affinity with any kind of weapon. Also, boost one of your attributes to superhuman capacity.

3 - You always find whatever you need to achieve your objective(s). Too bad having the right tools doesn't guarantee success.

4 - Until they see you in action, people tend to ignore and underestimate you.

5 - Your skill at tracking people through cities is beyond superhuman.

Recipe #305 – Murder Athlete Quiche Cups

1 - During a fight, you'll be able to ignore your injuries (from broken bones to fatal wounds) until the fight's over—then it'll all catch up to you. Note: certain injuries will still kill you on the spot (like decapitation or a nuke blast).

2 - #You're an athlete with peak human (maybe even superhuman) skill. What's your sport?

3 - #You're a well-versed killer. Your talents can be merely human or at superhuman capacity.

4 - You're famous (in a good way), which can come in handy—if you play your cards right.

5 - While you do need to sleep, you'll never become exhausted from sustained physical or mental activity.

Recipe #306 – Mystical Diplomat Egg Rolls

1 - For some reason, moral individuals tend to like you (even your enemies).

2 - For some reason, evil beings tend to like you (even your enemies). That's why they're more likely to spare your life or attempt to recruit you (even against your will).

3 - #Whether you're a genius or just pretty quick-witted, you often make very good decisions—to the point where people tend to follow you.

4 - You have the loyalty of a very dangerous being. Assign this individual three powers and a backstory.

5 - You have a useful network of mystical contacts.

Recipe #307 – Mystical Banker Cookies

1 - #You have a superhuman mastery of one non-mystical skill set (from doctor to pianist to CEO).

2 - You have your very own pocket dimension. Assign the rules, perks, and drawbacks to such a place.

3 - Certain places (oceans, battlefields, forests, etc.) actually boost your powers beyond superhuman, as long as you're physically present. Once you leave, the effect fades (set the details).

4 - #You can cast spells. How that works is up to you. Boost your Will attribute to superhuman capacity.

5 - You have easy access to a vast amount of previously stored information (what kind is up to you).

Recipe #308 – Nanoviral Chickpea

1 - #You can turn into a powdery being of some kind (like sentient snow, carnivorous alien death spores, nanites, etc.). If you wish, this can be your permanent form.

2 - You and/or your gear have a superhuman resistance to radiation (from dental X-rays to EMP attacks to spatial radiation).

3 - You can convert other beings into whatever you are (and pass along powers, skills, weaknesses, etc.). Anyone you train/turn is inclined to obey you.

4 - #You're some kind of robot. Boost three of your attributes to superhuman capacity.

5 - You can unleash a lethal plague. How does it work? Don't be afraid to mix it in with your other powers. Lastly, does it affect you?

Recipe #309 – Nanoviral Zombie Lab Spaghetti

1 - You have a secret lab with the resources to pursue your objectives.

2 - You can turn living beings into zombies. Also, feel free to mix this ability with another power(s).

3 - #You're a super genius with several non-violent skill masteries (set the details). Boost your Intellect to superhuman capacity.

4 - You can remotely hack into computers (via psychics, magic, etc.).

5 - You can control/remote-pilot your weapons, constructs, and gadgetry from far away—with superhuman skill.

Recipe #310 – Nerve Gas Caramel

1 - You have a chemistry skill that's beyond superhuman capacity.

2 - You can convert one type of gas into another. Set the details. Feel free to merge another power(s) with this one.

3 - You're immune to non-mystical toxins.

4 - You have a form-fitting field of solid air that's invisible to the naked eye and protects you from most attacks.

5 - #You're a genetic superhuman (born or augmented) with one free power and one superhuman attribute.

Recipe #311 – Nymphic Stout Cake

1 - #You are stunningly attractive and/or charismatic, which allows you to convince people to do whatever you want (at superhuman capacity).

2 - When you wish, normal people can't sense you. The effect ends if you attack someone or if someone views you through a device. Anyone with a superhuman Will (or the right powers) can also spot you.

3 - #Whatever you are, you can't pass for a human. Boost two of your human-scale attributes to superhuman capacity. Set the details on what kind of creature you are.

4 - #You're an anointed follower of a higher (or darker) power. Boost either your Will or Intellect to superhuman capacity. Needless to say, your prayers tend to get answered quickly (but in strange and mysterious ways).

5 - You have a number of lesser powers, which must be inspired by one of your other abilities.

Recipe #312 – Occult Architect Satay

1 - #Whether you're a genius or just pretty quick-witted, you often make very good decisions—to the point where people tend to follow you.

2 - #You're an alchemist with a finite number of potion formulas in your head. While they take time and materials to brew up, each potion's a temporary "power in a bottle." Set the perks and limitations.

3 - #You can enchant objects—both temporarily and permanently.

4 - #You have a superhuman mastery of one non-mystical skill set (from doctor to pianist to CEO).

5 - You have a useful network of mystical contacts.

Recipe #313 – Olive Oil Obliterator

1 - #Your Speed, Endurance, Might, and Health attributes are at the superhuman level. You can also self-regenerate by the minute.

2 - #You have alien blood in your veins. Boost two of your attributes to superhuman capacity.

3 - You have a noticeable organic armor that's permanently bonded to you (like a shell).

4 - You can unleash a focused explosive beam(s) with a significant range and superhuman damage. Can you reduce the damage?

5 - Get close enough to a living target and you can copy his/hers/its skills.

Recipe #314 – Onion Pie Growth Gun

1 - You can make living beings (but not yourself) grow to massive heights.

2 - You can undo the effect(s) of one of your other powers—unless it's too late.

3 - You have a potent, long-lasting, and self-recharging energy source. Set the details (including the blast radius).

4 - You can make objects grow.

5 - You have a one-of-a-kind, non-mystical weapon. You can wield it with superhuman skill. Its material strength is beyond superhuman capacity. Set the other details.

Recipe #315 – Onion-flavored Time Killer

1 - #You're a well-versed killer. Your talents can be merely human or at superhuman capacity.

2 - You can travel into the past and safely return. Set the details, ranges, and drawbacks.

3 - #You can't feel emotions of any kind. Boost either your Intellect or Will attribute to superhuman capacity.

4 - You can make other people forget meeting you, at superhuman capacity. The effect begins the moment they leave your immediate presence. Does this power have an "off" switch?

5 - You have a small arsenal of offensive and/or defensive gadgetry.

Recipe #316 – Pan Seared Biofeiter

1 - #You are—or were—a professional villain. Pick up a criminal skill specialty that you can utilize, with superhuman capacity.

2 - You can make temporary (and perfect) copies of any being you touch.

3 - If you wish, the corpses of your victims will vanish without a trace. Feel free to merge one/more of your other abilities with this one.

4 - Touch a corpse and you'll have its every memory and skill.

5 - #You're part of a hive mind. Set the details. Feel free to merge another relevant power(s) with this one.

Recipe #317 – Panfried Magic Whip

1 - You're a master of the whip, lariat, rope, chain, or any other melee attack that can entangle/lash.

2 - If you wish, your target won't be able to heal (or be healed) from weapon-based damage that you inflict. The effect lasts for days.

3 - The pain of others can heal you (by the second). Just inflict the pain or hang out near agonized beings.

4 - You're almost immune to all of your other powers (should they ever be used on you or somehow misfire).

5 - You've got an indestructible (mystical) item/weapon that'll return to you from anywhere. When wielding it, any feats you make are in the superhuman range. Any powers you merge with it will go beyond superhuman capacity.

Recipe #318 – Persuader Tacos

1 - You can persuade folks to do things your way with superhuman capacity.

2 - Your enemies never seek vengeance—unless they happen to run into you.

3 - #You're cursed to stumble into constant dangers that you must never avoid (or you will suffer).

4 - Anyone you successfully deceive will believe you (no matter what) until you personally confess to the lie.

5 - #You have accurate visions of the future. Set the details and limitations.

Recipe #319 – Pheromonal Demon Crockpot

1 - #You've got demonic blood in you. Pick up one extra power and boost two of your attributes to superhuman. Now, what kind of demon are you?

2 - #You can copy the appearance and voices of other humanoid beings.

3 - You can impregnate a living victim and expect one/more offspring within a number of hours. The rapid gestation will probably kill the host. Set the details on how this happened (sex, monster bite, mystical curse, viral sting, etc.).

4 - You can alter your clothing's size, shape, and appearance—but not its material strength. Set the details.

5 - You can release pheromones, which bend the wills (and sex drives) of others.

Recipe #320 – Plague Chops

1 - You've got an indestructible (mystical) item/weapon that'll return to you from anywhere. When wielding it, any feats you make are in the superhuman range. Any powers you merge with it will go beyond superhuman capacity.

2 - You can make a sacrificial offering to a higher being, in exchange for whatever you want. The bigger the "ask," the bigger your offering has to be-from favors to wealth to victims. Set the details. Feel free to merge another power(s) with this one.

3 - You can unleash a lethal plague. How does it work? Don't be afraid to mix it in with your other powers. Lastly, does it affect you?

4 - You can undo the effect(s) of one of your other powers—unless it's too late.

5 - Do a kill and your victims' life energies will flow into you and instantly heal some/all of your injuries.

Recipe #321 – Potion Archer w/ Bean Curd

1 - Whenever using a hand-held distance weapon, you'll never run out of ammo.

2 - #You're an alchemist with a finite number of potion formulas in your head. While they take time and materials to brew up, each potion's a temporary "power in a bottle." Set the perks and limitations.

3 - You have a one-of-a-kind, non-mystical weapon. You can wield it with superhuman skill. Its material strength is beyond superhuman capacity. Set the other details.

4 - Normally, it takes two actions to draw a weapon and then use it. Well, you're so fast that you can make it count as one action. If feasible, this advantage can also be applied to another power(s).

5 - You have some kind of variable-yield ammo (or possibly a power), which allows you to inflict different types of damage on a target. Examples would be gadget arrows, specialized bullets, or even assorted eye beams.

Recipe #322 – Primal Cutlet

1 - #You're a powerful minion who answers to Nature itself, via the element of earth. Pick up two extra powers that will help with your duties.

2 - This power allows you to talk to beasts and (usually) control them.

3 - You can call upon animals to serve you (from miles away). Does it work on mystical creatures (or hostile ones)?

4 - #Your skills at wilderness combat, survival, and tracking are at superhuman capacity.

5 - You can turn someone into an animal or a mutated variant of one. Set the details.

Recipe #323 – Psi-bateur Zucchini

1 - #You're a truly evil monster who must feed upon the living to survive. Boost two of your human-scale attributes to superhuman capacity.

2 - Establish contact and you can "drink" your victims' memories and skills away by the second.

3 - You can slap a temporary copy of your memories and skills into someone else's head.

4 - You have hundreds of skills in your head (maybe more).

5 - Somehow, you can give someone a copy of your skill set(s).

Recipe #324 – Psiggernaut Pizza

1 - You can reflect any psychic power or attack back to its point of origin. Is this power flexible enough to allow benign mental contact to get through?

2 - You can automatically sense the presence of psychic energies (and pinpoint the source) within a certain range.

3 - #You can turn into a metallic powerhouse with Might and Endurance attributes at superhuman capacity.

4 - Your overall physical dexterity is at superhuman capacity.

5 - If attacked by a mental power, you can temporarily copy it (assuming you survive). Set the other details, like how many powers you can safely contain.

Recipe #325 – Psi-legacy Mushrooms

1 - You can move solid objects, either via telekinesis or some kind of tractor beam.

2 - #You have alien blood in your veins. Boost two of your attributes to superhuman capacity.

3 - When you die, any of your innate powers and mystical items will automatically go to a pre-designated heir(s).

4 - #You have some kind of symbiote within your body (biological, psychic, tech-based, mystical, etc.). Feel free to merge your other power(s) with it.

5 - You can create a number of non-mystical barriers and forcefields, with flexibility on size and shape. How well do they protect against mystical attacks? Set the other details. Feel free to merge this ability with another power(s).

Recipe #326 – Psi-tutor Noodle Bake

1 - You have hundreds of skills in your head (maybe more).

2 - Somehow, you can give someone a copy of your skill set(s).

3 - You can indefinitely alter a target's entire worldview, with superhuman capacity.

4 - #You are—or were—a professional villain. Pick up a criminal skill specialty that you can utilize, with superhuman capacity.

5 - You can read and/or copy a target's memories, at superhuman capacity.

Recipe #327 – Pyro Warrior w/ Stuffing

1 - #You're a powerful minion who answers to Nature itself, via the element of fire. Pick up two extra powers that will help with your duties.

2 - Anything you wear or carry on your person can't be destroyed until you die or take it off—except for armor of any kind.

3 - You can create regular (or customized) archaic melee weapons out of thin air. Feel free to merge other powers with this one.

4 - Fire doesn't hurt you and can even heal your injuries, upon direct physical contact.

5 - You can summon a loyal being of solid energy (pick one type) with powers, skill masteries, etc. Set the details.

Recipe #328 – Rage Drug Ribs

1 - #You can just "snap" and plow into fights with a merciless rage and (temporarily) boosted Intellect. Do any other attributes increase to superhuman capacity? Will you only attack enemies, while enraged?

2 - You can go without eating, drinking, resting, or even sleeping for days at a time.

3 - You have access to an addictive drug. Set the details and feel free to merge them with other powers.

4 - During a fight, you'll be able to ignore your injuries (from broken bones to fatal wounds) until the fight's over—then it'll all catch up to you. Note: certain injuries will still kill you on the spot (like decapitation or a nuke blast).

5 - You can dodge almost any attack you see coming. It's the "un-dodgeable" attacks that you have to worry about (like a bullet to the back, an oncoming avalanche, etc.).

Recipe #329 – Rage Nuke Salad

1 - One of your OTHER powers is way beyond superhuman capacity and seems to have a mind of its own. How so?

2 - You can make everyone around you slip into a homicidal rage. Stay out of the fight and you'll be ignored. How does it work?

3 - In the presence of someone else's rage, you'll heal by the second.

4 - This power can make your victims violently hate anyone/anything you wish, at superhuman capacity.

5 - #You're playfully insane—until angered. Also, your mind's immune to mental intrusions of any kind. Boost your Endurance, Will, or Intellect to superhuman capacity.

Recipe #330 – Rage Weaver Tenderloin

1 - The presence of rage (either yours or someone else's) will temporarily boost your human-level attributes to superhuman capacity.

2 - Win a one-on-one fight and you can steal your foe's innate powers for 24 hours. How many powers can you safely hold at once?

3 - #You can't feel emotions of any kind. Boost either your Intellect or Will attribute to superhuman capacity.

4 - Your insults (no matter how trite) attack the mind with superhuman ability. Those who can't resist will drop everything and attack you.

5 - Extend the duration of another power's effect(s), if feasible.

Recipe #331 – Raisin Shocker

    1 - You can release focused electrical bolts from great distances.

    2 - You can hover (or outright fly) on currents of air.

    3 - #You can turn into solid energy (pick one type). If feasible, feel free to merge another power(s) into this one.

    4 - Any clothing you wear has a superhuman toughness, until you take it off.

    5 - Maintain contact (and concentration) with a device and you can power it up.

Recipe #332 – Rap Sorcerer Rouladen

1 - #You're a versatile musician-songwriter with a skill that's beyond superhuman.

2 - You're famous (in a good way), which can come in handy—if you play your cards right.

3 - #You can cast spells. How that works is up to you. Boost your Will attribute to superhuman capacity.

4 - You can automatically detect the presence of magic, within a certain range.

5 - You can heal from most injuries within a few minutes.

Recipe #333 – Refried Librarian

    1 - You can enchant an object, building, or place with warding magic. When triggered, the effects can vary. Usually, trespassers are contained, repelled, or injured in some fashion. Set the details.

    2 - #You don't age and will self-resurrect (if killed).

    3 - You've got a secret lair, with sufficient resources to pursue your objectives (whatever they may be).

    4 - You have a number of lesser powers, which must be inspired by one of your other abilities.

    5 - You have easy access to a vast amount of previously stored information (what kind is up to you).

Recipe #334 – Remote Gunner Pasta

1 - #You're a super genius with several non-violent skill masteries (set the details). Boost your Intellect to superhuman capacity.

2 - You can create high-tech weapons out of thin air.

3 - You can create small (non-weapon) devices out of thin air. With enough time (and skill), you can assemble components for a weapon or larger device.

4 - Any tech you make/own/use can (to a point) self-repair.

5 - You can control/remote-pilot your weapons, constructs, and gadgetry from far away—with superhuman skill.

Recipe #335 – Retired Fighter Jock Crockpot

1 - Whenever you're in a dangerous situation, you'll have unnaturally good luck—until the crisis ends. Then your luck returns to normal.

2 - #You're a cyborg, to the point where most of your body's been replaced with artificial components. Feel free to mix your other powers into this one. Are any of your attributes increased?

3 - You're famous (in a good way), which can come in handy—if you play your cards right.

4 - Your skill's beyond superhuman when driving or flying a vehicle—even for the first time.

5 - You have a unique, feature-loaded vehicle (from a spy car to an attack sub to a star cruiser).

Recipe #336 – Reusable Apocalypse Sandwich

1 - Merge this ability with any area-effect power/weapon you have. When using it, you can spare anyone or anything within its range (but nail everyone else). For this power to work, do you have to know where your "friendlies" are first?

2 - The souls of your victims end up your loyal slaves. Lay out the perks and limitations of this macabre ability.

3 - You can unleash a lethal plague. How does it work? Don't be afraid to mix it in with your other powers. Lastly, does it affect you?

4 - You've got an indestructible (mystical) item/weapon that'll return to you from anywhere. When wielding it, any feats you make are in the superhuman range. Any powers you merge with it will go beyond superhuman capacity.

5 - #You're an anointed follower of a higher (or darker) power. Boost either your Will or Intellect to superhuman capacity. Needless to say, your prayers tend to get answered quickly (but in strange and mysterious ways).

Recipe #337 – Rocky Road Dominatrix

1 - You can inflict overwhelming pleasure upon anyone you strike. How's that work?

2 - If you wish, anyone you personally injure (but don't kill) will instantly heal up.

3 - #You're meaner than most people. Boost your Endurance and Will attributes to superhuman capacity.

4 - You're famous (in a good way), which can come in handy—if you play your cards right.

5 - Your costume and/or uniform counts as lightweight body armor. Feel free to mix this power with any others you might have.

Recipe #338 – Rogue Amazon Cornbread

1 - You've mastered a number of potent curse enchantments that can be inflicted upon your targets.

2 - #You have extensive military experience and a natural affinity with any kind of weapon. Also, boost one of your attributes to superhuman capacity.

3 - #You're a world-class expert in the occult, with secrets worth killing for.

4 - #You are—or were—a professional villain. Pick up a criminal skill specialty that you can utilize, with superhuman capacity.

5 - Any weapon you use in a fight is unbreakable, as long as you wield it.

Recipe #339 – Rogue Android Sheet Cake

1 - #You're some kind of robot. Boost three of your attributes to superhuman capacity.

2 - You have a number of lesser powers, which must be inspired by one of your other abilities.

3 - You have hundreds of skills in your head (maybe more).

4 - #For every serious flaw you give yourself, you can pick up one free power.

5 - If you die, your body goes "BOOM." How severe is the blast?

Recipe #340 – Saboteur w/ Lime

1 - You can create short-range teleportation portals, through which you can spy, attack, flee, and/or maneuver.

2 - You can look at an object and know its structural status (including weak spots).

3 - Your skill with explosives is beyond superhuman capacity.

4 - You can design/build/operate any non-mystical device with a capacity beyond superhuman. However, it can't be a weapon.

5 - You have a small arsenal of offensive and/or defensive gadgetry.

Recipe #341 – Sacrificial Chamber Mousse

1 - You've got a secret lair, with sufficient resources to pursue your objectives (whatever they may be).

2 - You can put your victim's soul into an object (like a weapon, amulet, or coin). Anyone it touches can tap into that soul's memories, skills, or powers—pick one and set the details.

3 - Bad things happen to those who break an agreement with you. Feel free to mix another power(s) with this one.

4 - You can contact beings in other dimensions.

5 - You're well-versed in summoning mystical creatures (from other planes of existence).

Recipe #342 – Sautéed Shrimp & Storm Wielder

1 - You can control the weather. Set the range and other details for this power. Feel free to mix this with other (relevant) powers.

2 - #You're a powerful minion who answers to Nature itself, via the element of wind. Pick up two extra powers that will help with your duties.

3 - You can hover (or outright fly) on currents of air.

4 - Certain places (oceans, battlefields, forests, etc.) actually boost your powers beyond superhuman, as long as you're physically present. Once you leave, the effect fades (set the details).

5 - You have a form-fitting field of solid air that's invisible to the naked eye and protects you from most attacks.

Recipe #343 – Savior Fog Salsa

1 - You can create a dense, instant, and area-effect fog around yourself. Yeah, you can see through it just fine. Feel free to mix this with other (relevant) powers.

2 - #You're some kind of spectral entity (from a murdered soul to a possessive demon). Define your origins, strengths, and weaknesses.

3 - You can control a living target's body, like one would a puppet.

4 - For better or worse, your name is feared far and wide. Set the pros and cons of having such an infamous rep.

5 - You automatically sense when other people (within a certain range) are in danger, including enough details to interfere—if you want to.

Recipe #344 – Scrambled Multiplier

1 - You can create multiple, temporary copies of yourself.

2 - No matter how careless you are with your secret identity, no one can figure it out unless you intentionally reveal it.

3 - You can steal innate powers.

4 - You have a small arsenal of offensive and/or defensive gadgetry.

5 - Your costume and/or uniform counts as lightweight body armor. Feel free to mix this power with any others you might have.

Recipe #345 – Scrambler Venom Cupcakes

1 - You can inflict temporary amnesia on living minds. Set the details.

2 - You can fire a projectile that explodes on impact. Is the damage lethal or non-lethal?

3 - You have armor-piercing projectiles that can pump a desired drug/toxin into a target.

4 - You've got a poison that inflicts crippling pain upon superhumans who try to use their non-psychic, organic powers. The effect(s) are up to you.

5 - You have a poison that automatically kicks in if a target's INNATE psychic power(s) are used. The effect(s) are up to you.

Recipe #346 – See-thru Pistol Pops

1 - You can see through layers of inorganic matter without difficulty.

2 - Your distance attacks will harmlessly pass through the first solid object they hit (like a wall or body armor), then turn solid again. Set the details.

3 - You have some kind of variable-yield ammo (or possibly a power), which allows you to inflict different types of damage on a target. Examples would be gadget arrows, specialized bullets, or even assorted eye beams.

4 - You've got a mystical distance weapon that inflicts superhuman damage. Feel free to merge any of your other powers with it.

5 - You can see through organic matter (living or dead) with ease. Set the details.

Recipe #347 – Sidekick & Dumplings

1 - Nothing scares you. Period.

2 - #You're a genetic superhuman (born or augmented) with one free power and one superhuman attribute.

3 - You have a small arsenal of offensive and/or defensive gadgetry.

4 - Your costume and/or uniform counts as lightweight body armor. Feel free to mix this power with any others you might have.

5 - #You're a remarkable kid. How is up to you. Pick one attribute and boost it to superhuman capacity.

Recipe #348 – Signal Monster Hibachi

1 - Establish contact and you can "drink" your victims' memories and skills away by the second.

2 - You can send and receive communications signals over vast distances.

3 - #You're a truly evil monster who must feed upon the living to survive. Boost two of your human-scale attributes to superhuman capacity.

4 - One/more of your other powers can move through electronic devices (phones, radios, etc.) and affect someone on the other end.

5 - If you can establish psychic contact, this power will let you feed on a target's mind without having to be in the room. Whether it's for sustenance, to recover lost Health, or both is up to you.

Recipe #349 – Slow Cooked Villain

1 - #You're playfully insane—until angered. Also, your mind's immune to mental intrusions of any kind. Boost your Endurance, Will, or Intellect to superhuman capacity.

2 - Whenever you're in a dangerous situation, you'll have unnaturally good luck—until the crisis ends. Then your luck returns to normal.

3 - You have an extensive network of reliable criminal contacts.

4 - You always find whatever you need to achieve your objective(s). Too bad having the right tools doesn't guarantee success.

5 - For better or worse, your name is feared far and wide. Set the pros and cons of having such an infamous rep.

Recipe #350 – Smoked Cult Leader

1 - #Whether you're a genius or just pretty quick-witted, you often make very good decisions—to the point where people tend to follow you.

2 - You can make people fanatically loyal to you, with superhuman capacity.

3 - You've got a secret lair, with sufficient resources to pursue your objectives (whatever they may be).

4 - You have access to a loyal group of combat-hardened minions. Give them gear and an origin story (hired mercs, temporary conjurations, members of your tribe, etc.).

5 - During a fight, your attacks are always disturbingly efficient (possibly superhuman in scale). Your defensive and non-combat feats? Not so much.

Recipe #351 – Smoked Muscle

1 - #Your Speed, Endurance, Might, and Health attributes are at the superhuman level. You can also self-regenerate by the minute.

2 - You have an extensive network of reliable criminal contacts.

3 - Your skin's hardened against both physical and mundane energy attacks.

4 - #While you may take damage normally, only a handful of things can truly kill you. Boost your Will, Endurance, or Health attribute to superhuman capacity.

5 - You can throw non-weapon objects with a skill beyond superhuman. Whatever you can lift is fair game—from baseballs to lamps to crowded buses.

Recipe #352 – Smoked Pact Demon

1 - You can phase beings into yourself and lock them into a sort of stasis. During this time, you can access their powers, attributes, and memories. Set the limitations for this ability.

2 - #You've got demonic blood in you. Pick up one extra power and boost two of your attributes to superhuman. Now, what kind of demon are you?

3 - Bad things happen to those who break an agreement with you. Feel free to mix another power(s) with this one.

4 - You can persuade folks to do things your way with superhuman capacity.

5 - You can bless people with random good luck, which lasts for days at a time.

Recipe #353 – Smothered Spy

1 - #You have extensive military experience and a natural affinity with any kind of weapon. Also, boost one of your attributes to superhuman capacity.

2 - You have a perfect memory, capable of unlimited capacity.

3 - #Whether you're a genius or just pretty quick-witted, you often make very good decisions—to the point where people tend to follow you.

4 - #You are (or were) a spy, with a superhuman skill set.

5 - You cannot die, unless you allow yourself to be killed (say, via self-sacrifice).

Recipe #354 – Solar Knight Goat Cheese

1 - If immersed in flames, your Speed, Endurance, Will, and Health attributes will become superhuman. Hopefully, you're fireproof.

2 - You can safely exist in most hazardous environments.

3 - #You can turn into a being of solid, moving, fire. Set up the perks and flaws of this ability.

4 - If killed under sunlight, you'll quickly self-resurrect. Does ultraviolet light count? Set the details.

5 - You can fly. Set the details and feel free to merge another power(s) with this one.

Recipe #355 – Sour Cream & Demigoddess

1 - #You have the blood of a deity running through your veins. Boost one of your human-scale attributes to superhuman capacity and one of your powers beyond superhuman.

2 - You can turn one non-mystical liquid into another.*

3 - You can make one of your other powers' (temporary) effects permanent.

4 - You can get rid of one weakness/limitation within one of your other powers. However, you must replace it with a "replacement weakness/limitation" of some kind (your choice).*

5 - #You're an alchemist with a finite number of potion formulas in your head. While they take time and materials to brew up, each potion's a temporary "power in a bottle." Set the perks and limitations.

Recipe #356 – Sour Power Render

1 - Win a one-on-one fight and you can steal your foe's innate powers for 24 hours. How many powers can you safely hold at once?

2 - #You're a well-versed killer. Your talents can be merely human or at superhuman capacity.

3 - You can give a copy of one/more of your other powers (and optional weaknesses) to another being. How does that work?

4 - If you win a one-on-one fight, your defeated foe's innate powers won't work on you again—unless he/she/it beats you in a rematch.

5 - You can "see" the innate powers of anyone (or anything) you look upon.

Recipe #357 – Spectral Exorcist Melt

1 - #You're some kind of spectral entity (from a murdered soul to a possessive demon). Define your origins, strengths, and weaknesses.

2 - You know how to do exorcisms (whether by ritual magic, a mystical object, innate power, or some other means).

3 - #You're an anointed follower of a higher (or darker) power. Boost either your Will or Intellect to superhuman capacity. Needless to say, your prayers tend to get answered quickly (but in strange and mysterious ways).

4 - You can move solid objects, either via telekinesis or some kind of tractor beam.

5 - You can automatically detect the presence of magic, within a certain range.

Recipe #358 – Speedster Reporter Salad

1 - You're famous (in a good way), which can come in handy—if you play your cards right.

2 - #You're a speedster, which allows you to move at superhuman capacity (and probably faster than sound).

3 - You have a perfect memory, capable of unlimited capacity.

4 - You have a form-fitting field of solid air that's invisible to the naked eye and protects you from most attacks.

5 - #You have a superhuman flair for finding people and solving mysteries—whether you're a spy, lawman, freelance sleuth, or someone's pet enforcer.

Recipe #359 – Spiced Bodyguard

1 - You have some kind of kinetic beam attack. No, it doesn't do heat or explosive damage. It just pokes a hole through whatever it can penetrate.

2 - You have a form-fitting mundane forcefield, which offers you protection beyond superhuman capacity. Feel free to merge this power with other (relevant) ones.

3 - You never have to sleep.

4 - You can create a number of non-mystical barriers and forcefields, with flexibility on size and shape. How well do they protect against mystical attacks? Set the other details. Feel free to merge this ability with another power(s).

5 - You know the specifics of any ambush, just before it hits you.

Recipe #360 – Spicy CEO

1 - You have access to a reliable network of allies within business, government, and other legitimate sectors of society.

2 - #You are—or were—a professional villain. Pick up a criminal skill specialty that you can utilize, with superhuman capacity.

3 - #Somehow, you're very wealthy (probably with billions to your name).

4 - You have access to a loyal group of combat-hardened minions. Give them gear and an origin story (hired mercs, temporary conjurations, members of your tribe, etc.).

5 - No matter how careless you are with your secret identity, no one can figure it out unless you intentionally reveal it.

Recipe #361 – Sprinkled Metal Muscle

1 - You can safely exist in most hazardous environments.

2 - Your innate powers have a resistance to negation, theft, and manipulation that's beyond superhuman.

3 - #You're a genetic superhuman (born or augmented) with one free power and one superhuman attribute.

4 - If you consume metal while injured, you'll heal by the second.

5 - #You can turn into a metallic powerhouse with Might and Endurance attributes at superhuman capacity.

Recipe #362 – Spy Car Salesperson Muffins

1 - You can persuade folks to do things your way with superhuman capacity.

2 - #You are (or were) a spy, with a superhuman skill set.

3 - #You're a super genius with several non-violent skill masteries (set the details). Boost your Intellect to superhuman capacity.

4 - You have a number of lesser powers, which must be inspired by one of your other abilities.

5 - You've got a secret lair, with sufficient resources to pursue your objectives (whatever they may be).

Recipe #363 – Steamed Broccoli & Elven Symbiote

1 - #You have some kind of symbiote within your body (biological, psychic, tech-based, mystical, etc.). Feel free to merge your other power(s) with it.

2 - #You have enough elven blood to get the perks (attributes, longevity, etc.).

3 - #You're a genetic superhuman (born or augmented) with one free power and one superhuman attribute.

4 - You can make protective armor appear around you. Feel free to merge other powers into it.

5 - You've got a mystical melee weapon that inflicts superhuman damage. Feel free to add any of your other powers to it.

Recipe #364 – Stewed Tidal Terrorist

1 - Somehow, you can make liquids move (pretty much) however you want them to.

2 - You can breathe underwater and endure the depths of any ocean on Earth.

3 - Somehow, you can view a target (surroundings and all) from up to a certain range. Is this astral projection, magic, or something else? If relevant, you can mix this power with other abilities.

4 - You can move through the water disturbingly fast, for hours at a time. Hopefully, you have some way to breathe underwater.

5 - You can create and/or control tidal waves out of any (deep enough) body of water, at superhuman capacity. Set the details.

Recipe #365 – Strawberry Crooner Mage

1 - #You're a versatile musician-songwriter with a skill that's beyond superhuman.

2 - Only magic can harm you.

3 - #You can cast spells. How that works is up to you. Boost your Will attribute to superhuman capacity.

4 - #You have the blood of a deity running through your veins. Boost one of your human-scale attributes to superhuman capacity and one of your powers beyond superhuman.

5 - Someone (or something) is obligated to watch your back. This could be a bodyguard, demon familiar, loyal AI, etc.

Recipe #366 – Street Cyborg Mango

1 - #You're a cyborg, to the point where most of your body's been replaced with artificial components. Feel free to mix your other powers into this one. Are any of your attributes increased?

2 - #You are—or were—a professional villain. Pick up a criminal skill specialty that you can utilize, with superhuman capacity.

3 - You have a high-powered firearm of some kind, which does superhuman damage.

4 - Any tech you make/own/use can (to a point) self-repair.

5 - You have a small arsenal of offensive and/or defensive gadgetry.

Recipe #367 – Street Spy Pomelo

1 - #You are (or were) a spy, with a superhuman skill set.

2 - Your skill with disguises and impressions is beyond superhuman.

3 - #You have a superhuman flair for finding people and solving mysteries—whether you're a spy, lawman, freelance sleuth, or someone's pet enforcer.

4 - You always find whatever you need to achieve your objective(s). Too bad having the right tools doesn't guarantee success.

5 - You can persuade folks to do things your way with superhuman capacity.

Recipe #368 – Stuffed Dwarven Guardsman

1 - #You have enough dwarven blood to get the perks/limitations. What are they?

2 - The proximity of natural ground allows you to regenerate (from most injuries) by the second.

3 - #You have extensive military experience and a natural affinity with any kind of weapon. Also, boost one of your attributes to superhuman capacity.

4 - Your costume and/or uniform counts as lightweight body armor. Feel free to mix this power with any others you might have.

5 - You've got a mystical melee weapon that inflicts superhuman damage. Feel free to add any of your other powers to it.

Recipe #369 – Stuntbot Rillettes

1 - #You're some kind of robot. Boost three of your attributes to superhuman capacity.

2 - #You can copy the appearance and voices of other humanoid beings.

3 - You have hundreds of skills in your head (maybe more).

4 - Any tech you make/own/use can (to a point) self-repair.

5 - You have some kind of sensor tech that functions at superhuman capacity.

Recipe #370 – Sun-dried Time Traveler

1 - You can open a two-way communications link with someone in a different time period. Is this connection psychic, mystical, or tech-based?

2 - #You were born in a vastly different time period (past or future). Set the backstory.

3 - You have a unique, feature-loaded vehicle (from a spy car to an attack sub to a star cruiser).

4 - You have a small arsenal of offensive and/or defensive gadgetry.

5 - You can open a portal to any point in the past or future.

Recipe #371 – Super Diva Jailbait Sandwich

1 - #You can temporarily grow a bit taller and sprout extra muscles. Boost your Speed, Endurance, Might, and Health attributes to superhuman capacity. Set the details (including duration) and feel free to merge another power(s) with this one.

2 - #You're a remarkable kid. How is up to you. Pick one attribute and boost it to superhuman capacity.

3 - You can fly. Set the details and feel free to merge another power(s) with this one.

4 - Your skin self-hardens (like armor) just before anything harmful can hit you.

5 - Your costume and/or uniform counts as lightweight body armor. Feel free to mix this power with any others you might have.

Recipe #372 – Surfer Summoner Ragout

1 - You can move through the water disturbingly fast, for hours at a time. Hopefully, you have some way to breathe underwater.

2 - #Whether you're a genius or just pretty quick-witted, you often make very good decisions—to the point where people tend to follow you.

3 - Someone (or something) is obligated to watch your back. This could be a bodyguard, demon familiar, loyal AI, etc.

4 - You're well-versed in summoning mystical creatures (from other planes of existence).

5 - #You're a powerful minion who answers to Nature itself, via the element of water. Pick two free water-based powers.

Recipe #373 – Sweet Pepper Minion

1 - #You're meaner than most people. Boost your Endurance and Will attributes to superhuman capacity.

2 - No matter how careless you are with your secret identity, no one can figure it out unless you intentionally reveal it.

3 - Get close enough to a living target and you can copy his/hers/its skills.

4 - Your costume and/or uniform counts as lightweight body armor. Feel free to mix this power with any others you might have.

5 - You have a small arsenal of offensive and/or defensive gadgetry.

Recipe #374 – Teamwork Meatballs

1 - #You're a well-versed killer. Your talents can be merely human or at superhuman capacity.

2 - #You're part of a hive mind. Set the details. Feel free to merge another relevant power(s) with this one.

3 - If unconscious or in danger, your allies will get a "vision" of your plight and location.

4 - You have easy access to a vast amount of previously stored information (what kind is up to you).

5 - You can convert other beings into whatever you are (and pass along powers, skills, weaknesses, etc.). Anyone you train/turn is inclined to obey you.

Recipe #375 – Technosummoner Lettuce Cups

1 - You can remotely hack into computers (via psychics, magic, etc.).

2 - Your powers work in any and all dimensions.

3 - You're well-versed in summoning mystical creatures (from other planes of existence).

4 - One/more of your other powers can move through electronic devices (phones, radios, etc.) and affect someone on the other end.

5 - You have a number of lesser powers, which must be inspired by one of your other abilities.

Recipe #376 – Telekinetic Cannibal Truffles

1 - You can fly. Set the details and feel free to merge another power(s) with this one.

2 - You know the precise location of every living thing around you.

3 - #You can intimidate people with a superhuman capacity. When you get "scary," those with weaker minds might actually run away from you.

4 - #You're a truly evil monster who must feed upon the living to survive. Boost two of your human-scale attributes to superhuman capacity.

5 - You can move solid objects, either via telekinesis or some kind of tractor beam.

Recipe #377 – Telekinetic Minion Taters

1 - You answer to someone (or something) with a lot of useful connections and influence. This individual can ease your path, save your life, or have you killed for too many failures.

2 - You can make long-distance attacks, at targets you can't directly see, with a skill that's beyond superhuman capacity.

3 - You can move solid objects, either via telekinesis or some kind of tractor beam.

4 - #You're a well-versed killer. Your talents can be merely human or at superhuman capacity.

5 - Somehow, you can make liquids move (pretty much) however you want them to.

Recipe #378 – Teleportation Chimichangas

1 - You can teleport (with one passenger) across a certain range.

2 - You have some kind of sensor tech that functions at superhuman capacity.

3 - #You have extensive military experience and a natural affinity with any kind of weapon. Also, boost one of your attributes to superhuman capacity.

4 - You have a projectile weapon that fires sensor-filled ammo.

5 - You can teleport small objects to you, as long as they're within your power's range.

Recipe #379 – Teleporting Medic w/ Mushrooms

1 - Your skill at healing is beyond superhuman. This could apply to first aid, herbal medicines, formal medical practice, etc.

2 - You can accurately assess someone's injuries, diseases, and overall health with a glance. Feel free to merge another power(s) with this one.

3 - You have a suit of durable, self-mending armor. Feel free to fold your other power(s) into it.

4 - You can teleport (with one passenger) across a certain range.

5 - #You have an overwhelming need to do good—even if you're a benign crook. Boost two of your attributes to superhuman capacity.

Recipe #380 – Temporal Mastermind w/ Bacon

1 - You've got a secret lair, with sufficient resources to pursue your objectives (whatever they may be).

2 - #Somehow, you're very wealthy (probably with billions to your name).

3 - #You were born in a vastly different time period (past or future). Set the backstory.

4 - You have a small arsenal of offensive and/or defensive gadgetry.

5 - Your overall Intellect attribute is beyond superhuman capacity.

Recipe #381 – Three-cheese Mob Judge

1 - #You are—or were—a professional villain. Pick up a criminal skill specialty that you can utilize, with superhuman capacity.

2 - You'll automatically know if someone's lying to you.

3 - You have an extensive network of reliable criminal contacts.

4 - You have the loyalty of a very dangerous being. Assign this individual three powers and a backstory.

5 - For better or worse, your name is feared far and wide. Set the pros and cons of having such an infamous rep.

Recipe #382 – Three-headed Demon Danish

1 - Only magic can harm you.

2 - You have extra heads attached to you—each with its own brain and independent personality.

3 - You have a number of lesser powers, which must be inspired by one of your other abilities.

4 - Do a kill and your victims' life energies will flow into you and instantly heal some/all of your injuries.

5 - #You've got demonic blood in you. Pick up one extra power and boost two of your attributes to superhuman. Now, what kind of demon are you?

Recipe #383 – Throwing Sidekick Porridge

1 - You can throw non-weapon objects with a skill beyond superhuman. Whatever you can lift is fair game—from baseballs to lamps to crowded buses.

2 - You can make a distance attack that can hit multiple targets, either at once or in very rapid succession.

3 - You're able to make distance attacks that move/bounce around obstacles to hit a target. How does that work?

4 - #You're some kind of robot. Boost three of your attributes to superhuman capacity.

5 - With this power, you can make one guaranteed distance attack (per fight)—so make it count.

Recipe #384 – Timetalker Steak Fries

1 - #Your sonic attack inflicts sound-based and kinetic-force damage. Is it a yell, weapon, or something else? Feel free to merge it with other (relevant) powers/weapons.

2 - #You have some kind of symbiote within your body (biological, psychic, tech-based, mystical, etc.). Feel free to merge your other power(s) with it.

3 - You can send and receive communications signals over vast distances.

4 - You can open a two-way communications link with someone in a different time period. Is this connection psychic, mystical, or tech-based?

5 - #You are (or were) a spy, with a superhuman skill set.

Recipe #385 – Treasure Hunter Zucchini

1 - You have a small arsenal of offensive and/or defensive gadgetry.

2 - You have a secret lab with the resources to pursue your objectives.

3 - You have a unique, feature-loaded vehicle (from a spy car to an attack sub to a star cruiser).

4 - #You're a genetic superhuman (born or augmented) with one free power and one superhuman attribute.

5 - #You have a superhuman flair for finding people and solving mysteries—whether you're a spy, lawman, freelance sleuth, or someone's pet enforcer.

Recipe #386 – Tuscan Veal Armorer

1 - You can release an area-effect field that dampens one type of energy (mystical, psychic, or mundane). Pick it now, then set the details.

2 - #You have alien blood in your veins. Boost two of your attributes to superhuman capacity.

3 - You can create high-tech weapons out of thin air.

4 - Your battle armor protects you from damage and raises your Might attribute to superhuman capacity. What other features does it have? Feel free to merge another power(s) with this one.

5 - You have a suit of durable, self-mending armor. Feel free to fold your other power(s) into it.

Recipe #387 – Twice-baked Soul Slaver

1 - You can summon spirits of the dead. Set the perks and drawbacks.

2 - The souls of your victims end up your loyal slaves. Lay out the perks and limitations of this macabre ability.

3 - You can borrow a power from one of your offspring/minions (if applicable).

4 - You can make intangible spirits and mystical entities solid—either as a favor or to better fight them. Is this a temporary effect? Can you use this power on yourself? Set the details.

5 - You can put someone's deceased soul into a different corpse (and resurrect it). Feel free to merge this power with other (relevant) abilities.

Recipe #388 – Undercover Guard Bake

1 - You can sense the presence of threats and their general location(s).

2 - You can control a living target's body, like one would a puppet.

3 - Somehow, you can view a target (surroundings and all) from up to a certain range. Is this astral projection, magic, or something else? If relevant, you can mix this power with other abilities.

4 - From miles out, you can establish two-way telepathic contact with a handful of minds. Feel free to merge this power with other relevant abilities.

5 - You can read and/or copy a target's memories, at superhuman capacity.

Recipe #389 – Unstable Forcefield Focaccia

1 - You can safely release a 360-degree shockwave.

2 - You can unleash a focused explosive beam(s) with a significant range and superhuman damage. Can you reduce the damage?

3 - You can fly. Set the details and feel free to merge another power(s) with this one.

4 - One of your OTHER powers is way beyond superhuman capacity and seems to have a mind of its own. How so?

5 - You can create a number of non-mystical barriers and forcefields, with flexibility on size and shape. How well do they protect against mystical attacks? Set the other details. Feel free to merge this ability with another power(s).

Recipe #390 – Vampire Wizard Loaf

1 - #You're a predatory creature with unique dietary needs—but also some good left in you. Boost your Will and two other attributes to superhuman capacity.

2 - You can convert other beings into whatever you are (and pass along powers, skills, weaknesses, etc.). Anyone you train/turn is inclined to obey you.

3 - #You can cast spells. How that works is up to you. Boost your Will attribute to superhuman capacity.

4 - #While you may take damage normally, only a handful of things can truly kill you. Boost your Will, Endurance, or Health attribute to superhuman capacity.

5 - You have a number of lesser powers, which must be inspired by one of your other abilities.

Recipe #391 – Voodoobot Salsa

1 - If you can get a piece of the target and create a likeness, whatever happens to your "doll" happens to the victim.

2 - #You're some kind of robot. Boost three of your attributes to superhuman capacity.

3 - #You can copy the appearance and voices of other humanoid beings.

4 - You've mastered a number of potent curse enchantments that can be inflicted upon your targets.

5 - You're invisible to mystical detection, at a level that's beyond superhuman.

Recipe #392 – Wandering Monk Guacamole

1 - #Whether you're a genius or just pretty quick-witted, you often make very good decisions—to the point where people tend to follow you.

2 - You always find whatever you need to achieve your objective(s). Too bad having the right tools doesn't guarantee success.

3 - #You've mastered a mystical fighting style. That's why your fighting and acrobatic abilities are at superhuman capacity, along with your striking damage.

4 - Through meditation, you can heal your injuries (by the hour), figure out problems more easily, tolerate pain, and conserve oxygen.

5 - #You're cursed to stumble into constant dangers that you must never avoid (or you will suffer).

Recipe #393 – Warrior Statue Schnitzel

1 - #You can just "snap" and plow into fights with a merciless rage and (temporarily) boosted Intellect. Do any other attributes increase to superhuman capacity? Will you only attack enemies, while enraged?

2 - #You can turn into a metallic powerhouse with Might and Endurance attributes at superhuman capacity.

3 - You can create a dense, instant, and area-effect fog around yourself. Yeah, you can see through it just fine. Feel free to mix this with other (relevant) powers.

4 - For better or worse, your name is feared far and wide. Set the pros and cons of having such an infamous rep.

5 - Somehow, you can turn a flesh-and-blood victim into inanimate matter.

Recipe #394 – Watermelon Summoner

1 - You're well-versed in summoning mystical creatures (from other planes of existence).

2 - You can control a living target's body, like one would a puppet.

3 - You can permanently erase a fact from someone else's memories.

4 - You can banish beings from this dimension (even if they belong here). Set the details.

5 - Somehow, you can view a target (surroundings and all) from up to a certain range. Is this astral projection, magic, or something else? If relevant, you can mix this power with other abilities.

Recipe #395 – Whisked Barbarian Duelist

1 - You're famous (in a good way), which can come in handy—if you play your cards right.

2 - Your skill with a sword's beyond superhuman.

3 - #Your skills at wilderness combat, survival, and tracking are at superhuman capacity.

4 - #You have an overwhelming need to do good—even if you're a benign crook. Boost two of your attributes to superhuman capacity.

5 - You have a nigh-indestructible melee weapon. In your hands, does it inflict normal or superhuman damage?

Recipe #396 – White Chili Ancestral

1 - The second your firstborn draws breath, you'll stop aging and cannot die—until your last descendant dies. This could also apply to beings you create or "turn" (say, with a vampire's bite).

2 - No matter how careless you are with your secret identity, no one can figure it out unless you intentionally reveal it.

3 - You have access to a loyal group of combat-hardened minions. Give them gear and an origin story (hired mercs, temporary conjurations, members of your tribe, etc.).

4 - #You're an alchemist with a finite number of potion formulas in your head. While they take time and materials to brew up, each potion's a temporary "power in a bottle." Set the perks and limitations.

5 - #You've mastered a mystical fighting style. That's why your fighting and acrobatic abilities are at superhuman capacity, along with your striking damage.

Recipe #397 – Winged Armorer Hash Browns

    1 - You've got some kind of wings, which allow you to fly. Feel free to combine another power(s) into this one.

    2 - Your costume and/or uniform counts as lightweight body armor. Feel free to mix this power with any others you might have.

    3 - Your overall Intellect attribute is at superhuman capacity.

    4 - As long as you're moving around, incoming attacks tend to miss you. This power works at superhuman capacity—even on attacks you don't see coming. Of course, some attacks can't be dodged.

    5 - You have a number of lesser powers, which must be inspired by one of your other abilities.

Recipe #398 – Witch & Familiar Special

1 - You have the loyalty of a very dangerous being. Assign this individual three powers and a backstory.

2 - You have a useful network of mystical contacts.

3 - You have a mystical object that can boost one of your other powers beyond superhuman capacity.

4 - #You can cast spells. How that works is up to you. Boost your Will attribute to superhuman capacity.

5 - #You're an alchemist with a finite number of potion formulas in your head. While they take time and materials to brew up, each potion's a temporary "power in a bottle." Set the perks and limitations.

Recipe #399 – Womanizing Demigod Sauerkraut

1 - In your hands, any mundane weapon inflicts superhuman mystical damage. The effect ends right after you let the weapon go.

2 - Only magic can harm you.

3 - #You're meaner than most people. Boost your Endurance and Will attributes to superhuman capacity.

4 - #You have the blood of a deity running through your veins. Boost one of your human-scale attributes to superhuman capacity and one of your powers beyond superhuman.

5 - You can release pheromones, which bend the wills (and sex drives) of others.

Recipe #400 – Xenoshifter w/ Peanut Sauce

1 - #You have alien blood in your veins. Boost two of your attributes to superhuman capacity.

2 - #You can copy the appearance and voices of other humanoid beings.

3 - Without changing your overall appearance, you can alter your DNA, fingerprints, and other biometrics (well enough to fool sensors).

4 - You can surround your real memories with convincing fakes—at superhuman capacity—even if your mind's only human and a telepath's reading your thoughts.

5 - You can alter your clothing's size, shape, and appearance—but not its material strength. Set the details.

ABOUT THE AUTHOR

Marcus V. Calvert is a native of Detroit who grew up with an addiction to sci-fi that just wouldn't go away.

His goal is to tell unique, twisted stories that people will be reading long after he's gone. For him, the name and the fame aren't important. Only the stories matter.

You can find his novels, anthologies, and writing guides at:

*Website:
https://www.talesunlimited.net

*Facebook:
https://www.facebook.com/TalesUnlimited

CURRENT TITLES

Short Story Anthologies

The Unheroic Series

Unheroic: Book 1
Unheroic: Book 2
Unheroic: Book 3

The Book Of Schemes Series

The Book Of Schemes, Book 1
The Book Of Schemes, Book 2
The Book Of Schemes, Book 3

Novels

I, Villain Series

I, Villain
Murder Sauce
Frag Code
Coin Game

Writing Guides

The Batchery Series

Batchery, Volume I
Batchery, Volume II
Batchery, Volume III
Batchery, Volume IV

The Antagonists' Cookbook Series

The Antagonists' Cookbook, Vol. I
The Antagonists' Cookbook, Vol. II